QUAFFING
&
SCOFFING

Jilly Griffin

insight2foresight publishing

6 Burton Close

Wheathampstead

AL4 8LU

United Kingdom

Email: info@i2fpublishing.co.uk

First published 2016 © Jill Griffin

ISBN 978-1-909345-16-4

British Library Cataloguing-in-Publication Data

A catalogue record for this book is available from the British Library

Contents

How to Taste & Pair

The Drinks Pages

FOREWORD

I met Jilly for the first time in 2013. I was running some pairing dinners in a restaurant in London and she was left so impressed by the experience that she got in touch with our Association to get more information about us and our activity. One year after she enrolled for our full Certified Sommelier Course.

One of the most attentive, enthusiast and committed students of the course, Jilly was like a sponge, absorbing every new information with hunger for knowledge and an open mind.

As a Course Director and teacher, I am always extremely pleased when I am able to spot the enlightenment of passion in the eyes of my students. And Jilly was shining with enthusiasm! When she came to me telling me about the idea of writing a book about wine and food pairing (one of the subjects of my lectures) that was for me the cherry on top.

An ambitious project that a smart and determined woman put in practice in the best way possible: with her heart and soul. Say that I am proud of her it is an understatement. There's nothing better for a teacher to celebrate the success of his students, and it is a dream come true do be, even just a little, part of it.

But what fascinated so much Jilly? According to the Italian Sommelier Association pairing technique, the perfect marriage between food and wine is when flavours, aromas and sensations of both together, are able to create a third sensation that should be equal to, or better then the two singular taste of food and wine. You create something greater. You create. This is the most captivating aspect.

Using the skills learned applying the rules of pairing, and at the same time adding intuition, creativity and knowledge, a sommelier can create something new, something better, something unique. An exciting experience for our tasting buds, a challenge for our senses, an unrepeatable journey throughout aromas and tastes, enhancing the dining experience at the highest levels. And if you are a food and wine (and life) lover, you shouldn't ask for anything less!

All the best

Federica Zanghirella

Vice President & Course Director
UK Sommelier Association

INTRODUCTION

Just what do you drink with food at home?

When I studied and trained to be a sommelier with the UK Sommelier Association, I had to learn how to taste all over again. Identifying the aromas and individual tastes of food and drink took time. But little by little, my palate improved. I loved the course and the skills it gave me.

The pairings, understandably, were geared more towards restaurants and it didn't quite cover the British foods that I grew up with or the meals I eat at home today. In particular, that rainy Saturday lunchtime in November: the cupboards and fridge are pretty empty, yet your stash of wine is looking healthy: so just what do you drink with beans on toast? I decided to find out.

I did my preliminary research: most popular soups, sandwiches, take-aways, good old British fare, etc., and, based on my knowledge of analysing food and others' recommendations, made a short-list of possible pairings. There is so much information available on the Internet, it's hard to know what's what, but with a little care and attention, you can identify the useful, more reliable sites.

Next I gathered some food and wine aficionados together and we spent a season testing foods with the drinks I had short-listed. This book is the result of our tastings.

Perhaps I was inspired by a book I found when I lived in France: How to Cure Yourself with Wine. For every illness you could imagine, there was a French wine, to cure you miraculously. My partner at the time used to peruse the book, decide which ailment we should have that evening, and we'd drink the appropriate cure.

This book can help you in two ways. The front half of the book gives you the foods tested by The Taste Team with our preferred liquid refreshment in an easy-to-view format. The second half lists grape varieties and other drinks and suggests foods that will pair well.

I've also included a section on how to taste your drink and how to match your food with drink. You could carry out your own tastings and pairings with friends and family. Inevitably, there will be wine jargon and perhaps words you haven't come across before. Don't worry - there's a glossary at the end of the book.

The drinks I selected are readily available from supermarkets and independent wine merchants and the vast majority cost less than £14. I've described them in general terms, as I didn't want to restrict you by retailer, region, winemaker, or vintage. Some supermarkets have trained staff to give you advice. I would certainly recommend you establishing a relationship with a local independent vintner. Once they get to know you and your tastes, they can suggest wines you could try.

When all is said and done though, if you prefer a heavyweight Malbec with your prawns, go right ahead. It's your taste and your wallet. Yet when you find a truly harmonious pairing, it really does have that wow factor. Enjoy your food and drink.

Cheers!

THE TASTE TEAM

Come and meet the Taste Team.

I am very fortunate to have so many friends in the drinks industry. It was great that I could invite a group of people, all so very passionate about food and liquid refreshment, to take part in my experiments.

Not only did we learn a lot, but we had a blast at the same time, as well as some quite fierce debates. It wasn't all fun and games: I recall two consecutive evenings of tasting sweet things: about 120 mouthfuls of sugary foods. Maria, bless her, ended up in a fast food outlet for a bag of chips – just to have a savoury contrast.

Needless to say, I'm very grateful to the Team for giving up their time to help me. It was a fascinating project and I'm so pleased that I'm able to present the results.

Jilly Griffin
Food & Wine Devotee

Jilly's passion for food and wine matching started when she moved to France aged 21. Her friends Michel & Bernadette taught her all about French wine and French cooking.

Later in life, holidays always included wine hunting to fill her cellar and, when the trend for tasting menus and wine flights appeared, she was in her element.

For her own gratification, she qualified with the UK Sommelier Association, which concentrated largely on restaurant food.

As she's not allowed out much, Jilly wanted to discover what wines go with food that we typically eat at home. She decided to do more research and gathered together a mix of professionals and enthusiasts: because what do you drink with baked beans on toast?

Francis Giordanella
Wine Educator and Consultant

Francis has had a passion for food and wine that goes as far back as he can remember (and that is further than last week).

Coming from a continental background he can still recall all those wonderful and delicious mouth-watering aromas emanating from the kitchen and then the pairing with a good bottle of wine.

Francis is a qualified sommelier, and regularly takes part in wine paring events. He also writes articles for several wine magazines.

You can never know everything so Francis is still studying with the Wine Spirit Education Trust: his target being the Master of Wine accreditation. He is also a Freeman of the City of London and a Freeman of the Worshipful Company of Goldsmiths London.

Gojart "Arti" Reci

Arti is on the front line of food and wine matching. Currently Assistant Manager at the Ivy, Kensington, London, Arti has worked at the celebrated SixtyOne, Wild Honey in Mayfair, The Ivy in South Kensington London as well as restaurants in Italy.

Growing up in Siena, Italy, Arti found himself in the heart of Chianti country. This was where his passion for tasting food and wine started.

Learning the wine process and how fresh, seasonal food makes it to the table was instrumental in his choice of career and his studies with the Italian Sommelier Association. Arti is now embracing British food and the fusions it can lead to.

For Arti, it's not just the combination of food and drink that makes the meal, but the partnership with friends, family and good company to create a truly memorable experience

Maria Giancone
Food & Wine Writer

Maria's family moved from Sicily to Germany, where she grew up. Food and wine is as natural to her as walking her lovely dog Lollie.

In Italy, an accidental crossing of paths between Maria, with her marketing experience and language skills, and an Italian winemaker, allowed her entry into the world of wine. This move cemented her enduring love of wine.

Later, Maria worked for a co-operative of 52 wine makers in the Monferrato area of Piedmont, Italy. Maria's favourites are still Italian wines, and why not? Based in London these days, Maria is now a qualified sommelier.

Maria is working for a German wine magazine specialising in Italian wine and olive oil. Wunderbar.

Sean Poole
Wine & Food Aficionado

Hailing from down under, Sean entered the wine trade, as so many do, through mining in Madagascar. It was too easy to live the ersatz lifestyle of tropical tax havens, so he kept it real taking up enforced poverty looking for interesting things to do.

With a wine-making sister who now runs vineyards in the US, competition was always going to rear its head. His first foray went very well, management consultancy of a gorgeous Italian wine importer in London.

That led to management of on-line retailer Honest Grapes and then a cocktail of new English start-ups: Fishers Gin and Old Sport Whisky. A keen cook, astute palate, and dangerous on a dance floor, he can be found anywhere people are plying free food and drink.

Penny Sullivan
Wine & Food Fan

An(other) Australian in London who ended up with a job marketing wine almost by accident. Claims to be a wine novice, but has attended so many wine tastings, she's lost count.

Penny considered herself our layman on the Taste Team: she brought very few preconceptions to our tasting sessions (beyond a vague idea that white wine goes with fish), so when she said she liked a pairing: she liked it!

Having said that her opinion was just as valid as those with some technical knowledge. Penny continues to explore the world of wine and even dips her nose into the world of beer now and again.

Nick Ryman

Nick runs his own wine company, Maison Liedberg, specialising in the import and distribution of wine from boutique French wine makers. This must be the job of many people's dreams.

The mystique, the romance, the passion, the sheer emotion and care that goes into wine making fuels his interest. He particularly likes dealing with the smaller wine makers directly.

Nick always looks for wine makers whose main goal is to make the best possible wine that they can, given their environment, climate, terroir and just as importantly their own skill.

Nick has studied with the Wine & Spirits Education Trust and is a stalwart of the Central London Wine Society.

THE FOOD PAGES

BREAKFAST & BRUNCH

BREAKFAST & BRUNCH

Maybe your habit is just a strong coffee; tea and toast perhaps; maybe it's breakfast on the go; it might even be a cup of tea, then a second, perhaps even a third. Here are some typical breakfast bites I've tested. I've tried soft drinks for breakfast but added a tincture for when you fancy brunch a little later in the day.

A few notes:
- Drink strong coffee at the end of your meal otherwise it will overpower most foods;
- The strong acidity of most fruit juices will kill the delicate flavour of eggs and will taste sour with jams;
- Fruit juice, particularly orange, will work with sausages, hash browns, and black pudding and it'll cleanse your palate too.
- The winner for scrambled eggs is brut sparkling Wine. I mean brut English sparkling, Champagne or the Italian sparkler from Franciacorta. Prosecco and Cava have a touch of sweetness in comparison, which isn't such a good match.

"What about jams and marmalades?" I hear you cry. We didn't test these. It's a difficult one as the quality of preserves really does vary so much and the sweetness of some is just overwhelming. Home-made jams are a thing of beauty.

Marmalades have a bitterness as well as the sweetness. Should these contain any alcohol, then match it: e.g. marmalade with whisky (doesn't have to be neat: dilute to taste or the time of day).

A sweet sherry would work with both too as the persistence in the mouth would be similar. The sugar will make you thirsty and as we're usually dehydrated after a good night's sleep, why not make a full pot of tea too?

EGGS

Which came first the chicken or the egg?
Anon

> **The Food:** eggs: boiled, scrambled, poached, fried, omelette.
> **The Drink:** milk

Eggs are a delicate foodstuff. When the white and yolk are whipped up together, the result is light and creamy. The white on its own is smooth whereas the yolk can be runny or set. Toast has a slight sweetness, but the texture will differ from softer white bread to more dense wholemeal. The crunchiness of the toast will make a good contrast with the softness of the egg.

Food	Breakfast 1st	Brunch 1st	Brunch 2nd
Eggs Benedict	Cup of Tea	Brut sparkling wine	Wheat Beer
Fried Eggs	Watermelon Juice	Pinot Grigio	Wheat Beer
Hard Boiled Eggs	Milk	Pinot Grigio	Beer
Omelette	Milk	Brut Sparkling Wine	Sauvignon Blanc, e.g. Sancerre
Ham Omelette	Cup of Tea	Rosé	Beaujolais
Poached Egg	Watermelon	Pinot Grigio	Garganega, e.g. Soave
Scrambled Eggs	Milk	Brut sparking wine	Garganega, e.g. Soave

A note about omelettes: often omelettes will have a filling. The filling will have a stronger taste than the eggs so match your drink with the filling. With a ham and mushroom omelette, you could pair a young Pinot Noir.

Jilly from the Taste Team says:

A glass of cold milk with scrambled eggs: both are creamy and make good bedfellows.

OTHER BREAKFASTS

Breakfast like a king, lunch like a prince, dine like a pauper. Anon

The Food: toast, croissants, bacon, baked beans, waffles, anything that takes your fancy
The Drink: no clear winner see below

A good brekkie sets you up for the day. To start the day off with a great food and drink pairing is a joy indeed and puts a spring in your step. Breakfasts can be so varied: check the ones we tested below.

Food	Breakfast 1st	Brunch 1st	Brunch 2nd
Bacon Butty	Orange Juice	Côtes du Rhône	Cider
Beans on Toast	Milk	Côtes du Rhône	Cider
Croissant (Plain)	Hot Chocolate	Sauvignon Blanc	Soave
Full English	Orange Juice	Côtes du Rhône	Tawny Port
Mashed Avocado on Toast	Milk	Sauvignon Blanc	Wheat beer
Pain au Chocolat	Hot Chocolate	Moscato d'Asti	Tawny Port (chilled)
Peanut Butter	Coffee (not too strong)	Dessert Wine from Bordeaux (Sémillon based)	Tawny Port
Waffle	Milky Coffee	Sauvignon Blanc	Moscato d'Asti

Jilly from the Taste Team says:

A Full English is a great treat for me at the weekend, especially if someone else is cooking! A leftover glass of Tawny Port from the night before just hits the spot.

BRITISH SNACKS
&
LUNCHES

BRITISH SNACKS & LUNCHES

It was a joy to line up all our favourite British Snacks: the pork pie, sausage roll, pasty and the usual suspects.

I have a confession: I rather assumed you'd be more inclined to dip into this book rather than read it from cover to cover. If I'm wrong, you'll find out for yourself that some foods come under more than one entry.

Such a lot of choice for your lunch: as well as the traditional snacks we know and love, you'll find drink pairings for jacket potatoes, salads, sarnies and soups.

We enjoyed discovering which drink went well with each food. If you've found something better, do let me know, I'm on Facebook and Twitter. I'll be updating results and listing new pairings so please like Quaffing and Scoffing and follow @ Quaff_n_Scoff.

BRITISH SNACKS

Others might try to ridicule, but they don't have to eat it. No apologies here for our traditional fare. Jilly Griffin

> **The Food:** full of carbs: exercise beforehand.
> **The Drink:** Cider

No longer the preserve of the local garage's chilled counter, British snacks have been revitalised and now appear on the menus of high-end restaurants. Rediscover them for yourself. Most of these are perfect for picnics or lunch on the go. At work watch out for too many crumbs in your keyboard, it could play havoc with your colon.

Food	1st Choice	2nd Choice	3rd Choice
Bacon Buttie	Côtes du Rhône	Cider	Pinot Noir and Chardonnay, e.g. Chablis
Baked Beans on Toast	Côtes du Rhône	Cider	Milk
Cornish Pasty	Cider	Bitter	Pinot Noir
Pork Pie	Cider	Bitter	Chardonnay, e.g. Chablis
Sausage Roll	Cider	Bitter	Chardonnay, e.g. Chablis
Scotch Egg	Cider	Bitter	Côtes du Rhône
Welsh Rarebit	Cider	Bitter	Côtes du Rhône

Nick from the Taste Team says:

A touch of sweetness from the carbs is matched by the fruity cider, which was our overall winner. The bubbles cleanse the palate too.

JACKET POTATOES

What I say is that, if a man really likes potatoes, he must be a pretty decent sort of fellow. A A Milne

The Food: a potato baked in its skin, slit open, hollowed and refilled
The Drink: depends on the filling. See below

The trick is to get a crispy skin with a fluffy interior mixed with your filling of choice. It's the filling that determines which drink pairs best. Visually, it's not so great to just cut the spud in half, use the filling as a topping: it'll dribble and slide over the edges. Ignore the last sentence if you're ravenous of course!

Jacket potato with:	1st Choice	2nd Choice	3rd Choice
Baked Beans	Côtes du Rhône	Chianti Classico	Rioja
Bolognese Sauce	Chianti Classico	Rioja	Barbera
Cheese	Chardonnay	Bardolino	Milk
Chilli con Carne	Rioja	Chianti Classico	Malbec
Coleslaw	Milk	Rosé	Bardelino
Coronation Chicken	Perry	Wheat Beer	Chenin Blanc (South Africa)
Roasted Veg	Chianti Classico	Chenin Blanc	Perry
Tuna & Sweetcorn	Gin & Tonic	Lightly oaked Chardonnay from Chile	Perry

A jacket potato is a great way to use up leftovers: Bolognese, Roasted Veg, etc.

Jilly from the Taste Team says:
The potato will add a slight sweetness to the mix. Base your drink on the filling – it will be the dominant character.

SALADS

Celebrity spotting in London restaurants is a fine sport. Yet you'll never see Sir Elton John eating a Caesar Salad ...... because he's a Rocket Man. Boom Boom. Anon

The Food: a mix of leaves, veg, dressing perhaps with meat or fish
The Drink: varied. See below.

It's easy to consume a few of your five-a-day when you eat a salad. It can be your filling or slimming main course, a tasty starter or a simple side. When I had a kitchen garden, I used to grow all my own salads. These days though it's so much easier to buy the ready-prepared, pre-washed salads in a bag.

Salad	1st Choice	2nd Choice	3rd Choice
Chicken & Bacon Pasta	Picpoul de Pinet	Sauvignon Blanc	Wheat Beer
Chicken Caesar	Unoaked Chardonnay	Bordeaux Rosé	Sauvignon Blanc
Cous Cous	Picpoul de Pinet	Sauvignon Blanc	Perry
Ham Hock, Egg & Potato	Unoaked Chardonnay	Sauvignon Blanc	Lager
Plain Green	Orvieto	Chardonnay	Wheat Beer
Prawn Cocktail	Picpoul de Pinet	Orvieto	Torrontés
Rocket & Poached Salmon	Picpoul de Pinet	Unoaked Chardonnay	Perry
Rocket & Spicy Poached Salmon	Perry	Torrontés	Picpoul de Pinet
Salade Niçoise	Rosé	Chenin Blanc	Picpoul de Pinet
Tomato & Mozzarella	Torrontés	Riesling	Rosé
Waldorf	Cider	Torrontés	Chenin Blanc

Penny from the Taste Team says:

Pairing with dressings can be a problem: vinaigrette is acidic and this will conflict with any wine. Try using what you're drinking instead of the vinegar or using the sweeter balsamic vinegar, sherry or even fruit juice.

SARNIES

Too enthralled to leave a game of poker, John Montagu, the 4th Earl of Sandwich asked for a slice of meat stuffed between two slices of bread. A British staple was born.

The Food: a vast choice of fillings inside a roll, slices of bread (white, brown, wholemeal, rye, spelt bread, seeded), crackers, pitta.
The Drink: perhaps Perry but check below.

The choice of bread will make a difference to the texture in your mouth and the taste. A wholemeal bread for example will be chewier, and feel fuller in the mouth as well as adding a cereal taste; so it will take on a fuller-bodied, stronger-tasting drink. Soft white bread that almost melts in the mouth needs something more delicate, depending on the filling.

Sarnie	1st Choice	2nd Choice	3rd Choice
Bacon Butty	Côtes du Rhône	Cider	Orange Juice
BLT	Sauvignon Blanc	Lemon Ice Tea	Languedoc Grenache
Beef & Horseradish	Sauvignon Blanc	Tawny Port	Languedoc Grenache
Cheese & Branston	Perry	Riesling	Belgian White Wheat Ale
Chicken & Bacon	Perry	Riesling	Belgian White Wheat Ale
Chip Butty	Cider	Riesling	Grüner Veltliner
Chip Butty with Ketchup	Riesling	Cider	Grüner Veltliner
Coronation Chicken	Perry	Lemon Ice Tea	Viognier
Cucumber	Gin & Tonic	Lemon Ice Tea	Côtes du Rhône Rosé
Egg & Cress	Gin & Tonic	Perry	Lemon Ice Tea

Sarnie	1st Choice	2nd Choice	3rd Choice
Fish Finger Sandwich	Cider	Brut Sparkling English wine	Riesling
Ham & Mustard	Languedoc Grenache	Lemon Ice Tea	Sauvignon Blanc
Marmite & Watercress	Sauvignon Blanc	Lemon Ice Tea	Tawny Port
Prawn Mayo Sandwich	Perry	Riesling	Lightly oaked Chardonnay from Chile
Smoked Salmon & Cream Cheese Sandwich	Perry	Riesling	Lightly oaked Chardonnay from Chile
Tuna & Sweetcorn	Gin & Tonic	Lightly oaked Chardonnay from Chile	Perry

If you're adding relish, pickles, chutneys, mustard, etc., this condiment could overpower the filling. Match your drink to the condiment.

Vinegar in pickles and chutneys is a killer for wine, in particular, and will result in an unpleasant aftertaste. Sip your drink after a bite of the crust so that any vinegar residue is smaller in proportion to the mouthful.

Sweet or spicy condiments need a smooth, sweet drink. This doesn't necessarily mean sugary sweet. Some wines smell and taste so fruity that you think they're sweet, when actually they're dry.

Nick from the Taste Team says:

Gin & Tonic was a revelation but went surprisingly well with some of the sandwiches. It was a damn good G&T: posh tonic and the gin with cucumber botanicals.

SOUPS

"I could dance with you till the cows come home. On second thoughts, I'd rather dance with the cows till you come home."
Rufus T. Firefly, Duck Soup

> **The Food:** a liquid dish, usually served warm.
> **The Drink:** perhaps Perry but sometimes it didn't rank at all. See below

Hot, cold, thick, thin, soups are perfect for Bonfire Night, camping, and easy lunches. We tested readily available soups from the supermarket. You can tweak your soups by adding extra ingredients, e.g. fried bacon to a butternut squash soup. Just remember to match your drink with the strongest flavour.

Soup	1st Choice	2nd Choice	3rd Choice
Butternut Squash	Perry	Gin & Tonic	Lemon Ice Tea
Carrot & Coriander	Gin & Tonic	Tawny Port	Lemon Ice Tea
Curried Parsnip	Perry	Lemon Ice Tea	Gin & Tonic
French Onion	Sauvignon Blanc	Grenache from Languedoc	Frascati
Leek & Potato	Perry	Lightly oaked Chardonnay from Chile	Côtes du Rhône Rosé
Lobster Bisque	Gin & Tonic	Tawny Port	Lemon Ice Tea
Minestrone	Perry	Riesling	Lightly oaked Chardonnay from Chile
Mulligatawny	Perry	Lightly oaked Chardonnay from Chile	Riesling
Mushroom	Perry	Riesling	Lightly oaked Chardonnay from Chile
Oxtail	Grenache from Languedoc	Sauvignon Blanc	Lemon Ice Tea

Soup	1st Choice	2nd Choice	3rd Choice
Pea & Ham	Perry	Belgian White Wheat Ale	Riesling
Tomato	Grenache from Languedoc	Lemon Ice Tea	Porter

Francis from the Taste Team says:

Lemon Ice Tea was the surprise contender here. The commercial variety was rather sweet and we'd like to retry with a home-made version.

BRITISH CLASSICS
&
MAINS

BRITISH CLASSICS & MAINS

The drinks we tested throughout our tastings are readily available at supermarkets. If it's a special occasion though, you might like to go a bit more upmarket. If your local supermarket doesn't stock what you want, ask them to get it; visit your local independent merchant; or buy on line.

Many British Classics seem to be relegated these days to the counties or regions whence they came. This is a real shame yet, with chefs always looking for something new , maybe these dishes will be fashionable again soon.

The classics we tested are readily available in supermarkets too – because that's where most of us shop. If you're making a dish from scratch, it's likely to be more flavoursome so you might need to adjust the drink accordingly and choose something more complex, older or from a better winemaker.

Try a more complex wine: this could be a blend, an older vintage and/or a more renowned winemaker.

Main courses tend to be the principal meal of the day, whether it's at lunchtime or in the evening. Here's your opportunity to stock up on your five-a-day. Most vegetables have a slight sweetness about them and will complement the acidity in a drink.

Some veggies are reputedly a little harder to match, e.g. sprouts, asparagus, artichoke. If you've matched your drink to the meat, then take a sip after the meat and not the veg.

BBQs

My meat is hand rubbed, well seasoned, aged to perfection and always hot. Anon

The Food: fish, meat, veg and cheese, cooked over a source of heat.
The Drink: varies but this is a time for your big reds!

Part of the summer dream: sunny weather, good company, salads, meats, fish, veg and cheese cooking over a flame, charcoal or smoke. More likely it'll be cold, perhaps the odd shower, flames and burnt bits. If there's a crowd, this is when your screw-capped wines come into their own. Pick crowd-pleasing drinks rather than your best bottles. Offering too many drinks will make it more difficult to calculate quantities: try a white and red wine, a beer and a soft drink. If it's 40°C in the shade, a Malbec at 14% might be a little powerful and a beer more refreshing.

Food	1st Choice	2nd Choice	3rd Choice
Burgers	Cider	Pinot Noir	Cabernet Sauvignon
Chicken	Unoaked New World Chardonnay	Picpoul de Pinet	Wheat Beer
Chops - lamb	Shiraz	Californian Zinfandel	Rosé
Chops - pork	Cider	Pinot Noir	New World Riesling
Halloumi	Dry Bordeaux White (Sémillon/Sauvignon Blanc)	Unoaked New World Chardonnay	New World Riesling
Ribs	Californian Zinfandel	Malbec	Cabernet Sauvignon
Salmon	New World Riesling	Unoaked New World Chardonnay	Pinot Noir
Sausages	IPA	Rioja	Californian Zinfandel
Seafood Kebabs	Unoaked New World Chardonnay	Rosé	Lightly chilled Pinot Noir

Food	1st Choice	2nd Choice	3rd Choice
Steak	Syrah	Malbec	Californian Zinfandel
Veggie Kebabs	Unoaked New World Chardonnay	Pinot Noir	IPA

The taste test above was on fairly plain foodstuffs. If you're using a strong marinade or accompanying sauce, match your drink to that.

Here are some tips:
- Burnt bits have a slightly bitter taste: the more burnt it is, the fruitier, smoother and even sweeter the drink you need
- Lots of herbs can also result in a slightly bitter taste: fruity, smooth and sweet is the answer.
- Hot and spicy: guess what? Fruity, smooth and sweet.
- Chill your reds for 20 mins, especially light reds, before serving
- Wines from hotter climes (Australia, Chile, California, and the Med) tend to taste riper and fruitier.

Jilly from the Taste Team says:

If it's chilly, and maybe just a few of you, sip a port for a treat

BRITISH CLASSICS

Food glorious food
Hot Sausage & Mustard!
Song from Oliver, by Lionel Bart

The Food: meat or fish combined with carbs
The Drink: varied, see below.

The following results are for some of the classic British dishes I grew up with. Hearty food that suited an active lifestyle and the chilly weather and there's nothing wrong with that. Most of these dishes appear again under separate headings.

Food	1st Choice	2nd Choice	3rd Choice
Bangers & Mash (Pork Sausages)	Grüner Veltliner	Dry Riesling	Cider
Cottage Pie	Syrah	Rioja Reserva	Chianti Classico and Bardolino
Fish & Chips	Brut Sparkling English wine	Riesling	Cider
Fish Cakes	Chardonnay (lightly oaked or, if there's spice, unoaked)	Picpoul de Pinet	Wheat Beer
Fish Pie	Chenin Blanc	Lightly oaked Chardonnay	Picpoul de Pinet
Roast Chicken Pie	Bardolino	Chianti Classico	Rioja Reserva
Shepherd's Pie	Rioja Reserva	Syrah	Bardolino
Steak & Mushroom Pie	Bardolino	Chianti Classico	Syrah
Toad in the Hole (Pork Sausages)	Bardolino	Chianti Classico	Cider

Our traditional dishes, more comforting even than school dinners, work both for a tasty midweek meal and a more special occasion at the weekend. To upgrade, either use better ingredients in the food or a more expensive drink: e.g. fish 'n' chips with cider during the week, but at the weekend, crack open a bottle of fine English sparkling wine.

Jilly from the Taste Team says:
Comfort food, when paired with the right drink, morphs into a thing of beauty. Cheers!

FISH & SHELLFISH

Give a man a fish and he has food for a day; teach him how to fish and you can get rid of him for the entire weekend.
Zenna Scha

The Food: seafood treasures
The Drink: whites dominate in this section.

Fish and shellfish always remind me of summer. Lemon is often provided on the plate to be squeezed over your seafood. Please don't squeeze. The theory of lemon's acidity with seafood is good, but let your wine's acidity take charge instead.

Food	1st Choice	2nd Choice	3rd Choice
BBQ Seafood Kebabs	Unoaked New World Chardonnay	Rosé	Lightly chilled Pinot Noir
BBQ Salmon	New World Riesling	Unoaked New World Chardonnay	Pinot Noir
Fish & Chips	Brut Sparkling English wine	Riesling	Cider
Fish Cakes	Chardonnay (lightly oaked or, if there's spice, unoaked)	Picpoul de Pinet	Wheat Beer
Fish Goujons	Brut Sparkling English wine	Riesling	Cider
Fish Pie	Chenin Blanc	Lightly oaked Chardonnay	Picpoul de Pinet
Prawns	Dry Fino Sherry	Vermentino	Wheat Beer
Salmon Fillet	Rosé	Lightly oaked Chardonnay	Dry Riesling
Salmon en Croûte	Chardonnay	Riesling	Sauvignon Blanc
Sushi	Saké	Pinot Gris	Riesling

We didn't test each and every fish so here are some tips to guide you:

- The dominating flavour with white fish is often the sauce that goes with it. Match your drink to the sauce:
  ◇ Sweet and sour: perry
  ◇ Teriyaki: Saké, off-dry Riesling
  ◇ Herby: Torrontés, Perry
  ◇ Creamy: Chardonnay
- Meaty fish, such as swordfish and tuna, can handle red wines: Pinot Noir, Beaujolais, especially chilled
- Seafood has a slight sweetness which makes a good pairing with the acidity in a wine, e.g. Vermentino
- The classic pairing for Oysters is Stout, but if you prefer wine then try:
  ◇ Chardonnay from Chablis;
  ◇ Stuffed oysters with breadcrumbs: brut sparkling wine;
  ◇ Oysters in a creamy sauce: Chardonnay;
  ◇ Vinegar, Tabasco, or lemon: stick to water!
- With mussels:
  ◇ If alcohol's in the sauce, drink that too, e.g. Moules Marinières with Muscadet from the Loire in France
  ◇ Creamy mussels: Chardonnay or even a cider
  ◇ Mussels in a tomato sauce: Bardolino or Chianti Classico
  ◇ Mussels with a breaded crumb: sparkling wine

Francis from the Taste Team says:
Plainly cooked fish and seafood need delicate wines otherwise the pairing will be unbalanced and the food will be overpowered.

PIES

Skinny people are easier to kidnap. Eat more pies! Sign outside Fullers' The Admiralty pub on Trafalgar Square, London.

> **The Food:** moist filling enrobed in pastry or topped with mash.
> **The Drink:** syrah for the meats

Pies: comfort food par excellence. Nothing quite like it on a chilly day. Meaty pies are a great way of using up leftovers too.

Fish pie on the other hand can be mid-week value or, with the addition of salmon, quails eggs, scallops, and any other choice pieces, a luxurious dinner party dish. The latter will need a fuller white wine to go with it: a Californian or Burgundian oaked Chardonnay, with some malolactic fermentation (sorry: went technical there – see the Glossary for an explanation).

Pie	1st Choice	2nd Choice	3rd Choice
Cottage Pie	Syrah	Rioja Reserva	Chianti Classico and Bardolino
Cumberland	Syrah	Rioja Reserva	Chianti Classico
Fish	Chenin Blanc	Lightly oaked Chardonnay	Melon de Bourgogne, e.g. Muscadet from the Loire, France
Pork	Cider	Bitter	Chardonnay, e.g. Chablis
Roast Chicken	Bardolino	Chianti Classico	Rioja Reserva
Shepherd's	Rioja Reserva	Syrah	Bardolino
Steak & Mushroom	Bardolino	Chianti Classico	Syrah

Penny from the Taste Team says:

It was interesting to note that the supposedly food friendly red wines, Chianti, Rioja, Bardolino, really are just that!

SUNDAY ROASTS

Sundays: sleep until you're hungry; eat until you're sleepy. Anon

> **The Food:** whole birds or big lumps of meat roasted in the oven
> **The Drink:** bring out your reds!

There's nothing quite like a Sunday roast. The smells, the anticipation, laying the table, serving, stuffing your face, clearing up (or leaving it until later), slumping, looking forward to next time.

Some roasts might have a basting of something sweet or spicy. If so, alter your wine to smooth, fruity and off-dry: Riesling, Chenin Blanc, from Vouvray in the Loire, France.

If your gravy or sauce is made with wine or beer, drink that with the food too.

Roast	1st Choice	2nd Choice	3rd Choice
Beef	Côtes du Rhône or GSM mix (Grenache, Syrah, Mourvèdre)	Bordeaux Blend	Porter
Chicken	Pinot Noir	Oaked Chardonnay	Cider
Duck	Nebbiolo (Barolo)	Zinfandel	Côtes du Rhône
Ham	Chianti Classico	Merlot	Cider
Lamb	Bordeaux Blend	Rioja Reserva	Cabernet Sauvignon
Pheasant	Pinot Noir	Chianti Classico	Merlot
Pork	Pinot Noir	Chenin Blanc	Cider
Turkey	Pinot Noir	Oaked Chardonnay	GSM or Côtes du Rhône

We didn't test the following, but here are my recommendations nonetheless:

Roast	1st Choice	2nd Choice	3rd Choice
Goose	Nebbiolo (Barolo)	Côtes du Rhône / GSM Blend	Côtes du Rhône
Rabbit	Pinot Noir	Chianti Classico	Merlot
Venison	Nebbiolo (e.g. Barolo)	Zinfandel	Côtes du Rhône / GSM blend
Wild Boar	Malbec	Cabernet Sauvignon	Porter

Some extra tips:

- If you're barding your meat with bacon, avoid tannic wines. Salty tastes and tannins will clash.
- With a redcurrant relish, cranberry sauce, or other condiment, keep to a soft, fruity wine, low in tannins.
- Oaky wines with low-fat meat will dry out your mouth, leaving an unpleasant mouthfeel. Add extra moisture through gravy and sauces.

Sean from the Taste Team says:

This is red wine territory: wines with tannins will go better with fattier meats and stews and casseroles.

TAKE-AWAYS

TAKE-AWAYS

I've split our results into different cuisines, so you'll find here:

- American
- British
- Chinese
- Indian
- Italian
- Thai

A take-away can save us time, might be better than we could make ourselves (practise makes perfect so I'm quite happy for the experts to prepare my curry), and the supermarket take-away aisles are full of meals to heat up at home.

If you're aiming for something spicy, here are some general tips:

- Alcohol will enhance hot spices, so try to keep the abv down a bit
- Avoid tannic wines with fiery spices
- Choose a drink that has a sweetness to it in order to calm any fierce flavours
- Insipid drinks won't stand up to fiery food.

Otherwise usual guidelines apply:

- Match food weight with the body of the wine
- Acidity cuts through fats
- Length of flavour in the mouth should be roughly the same between the dish and the drink

AMERICAN

I'm lovin' it.
McDonalds.

The Food: fatty and salty with umami. American classics.
The Drink: IPA was the most popular but it seems anything goes.

A lot depends on the toppings and condiments that you add. We all have our own favourites. But there's no denying that these foods are fatty and salty – both characteristics play havoc with your taste buds. To counteract this, go for lowish ABV, carbonation and some residual sugar. A beer's hops will cut through the fat. Bubbles, from beer or wine, will cleanse the palate between mouthfuls.

Food	1st Choice	2nd Choice	3rd Choice
Burger	Cider	Pinot Noir	Cabernet Sauvignon
Cheeseburger	IPA	Riesling	Pinot Noir
Fried Chicken	IPA	Sparkling Wine	Moscato d'Asti
Hot Dog (with mustard mayo)	IPA	Rosé	Pinot Noir

Sean from the Taste Team says:

Stuffing your face with a burger and a beer in New York City: it should be on everyone's bucket list, followed by a long, hard look at your list.

BRITISH

The Food: fish deep fried in batter with large cut chips.
The Drink: if you can afford it english sparkling wine!

Remember eating fish & chips at the seaside? The parrot-like question of "Salt 'n' vinegar?" Wrapped in newspaper (which stopped in 1980) or not, it's such a tradition that it's said you should only eat fish & chips in sight of the sea. I wouldn't go as far as that: I reckon they're a favourite wherever you are.

Food	1st Choice	2nd Choice	3rd Choice
Fish & Chips	English Sparkling Wine	Dry Riesling	Grüner Veltliner
Chip Butty	Cider	Dry Riesling	Grüner Veltliner
Chip Butty with Ketchup	Dry Riesling	Cider	Grüner Veltliner

Fish & Chips has dropped down the league table of most popular take-aways (behind Indian, Chinese and pizzas) but they're still a top item on the menu of nearly every pub in the UK. The fish is battered and deep fat fried from the chippy but may be bread-crumbed elsewhere, and the chips are proper fatties not matchsticks. Cod is still the top seller but haddock, pollock, coley, plaice, skate ray and huss can be found too. In January each year, the National Fish & Chips Awards are given out.

Nick from the Taste Team says:

This is where you have to refuse the vinegar and keep the lemon as decoration. The combination is good but by adding acidity to cut through the oiliness, you're losing the crispy texture and crunch in the mouth. Use the acidity of your drink instead.

CHINESE

"I just love Chinese food. My favourite dish is number 27." Supposedly Clement Atlee, former British Prime Minister

> **The Food:** rice or noodle based, with vegetables, fish or meat. Different regional styles but sometimes only a Chinese will hit the spot.
> **The Drink:** riesling

Chinese food is as varied as the country is vast. Often the cuisine is adapted to suit the tastes of the host country. It's said that you're hungry again an hour after eating a Chinese. The Chinese would counter that you should always leave the table knowing you could eat a little more.

Food	1st Choice	2nd Choice	3rd Choice
Aromatic Crispy Duck	Riesling	Perry	Fruity Rosé
Chicken & Cashew	Riesling	Perry	Torrentés
Crispy Beef	Chinese Beer	Perry	Riesling
Ginger Beef	Gewürztraminer	Pinot Grigio and Perry	Californian Pinot Noir
Singapore Noodles	Torrentés	Riesling	Fruity Rosé
Sweet & Sour Pork	Perry	Riesling	Fruity Rosé

Penny from the Taste Team says:

This bog standard supermarket Riesling was our winner, especially for a meal of different dishes.

INDIAN

Keep korma and curry on.
Anon

> **The Food:** diverse regional dishes from across India: easy for vegetarians to find something choice
> **The Drink:** wheat beer.

We've come a long way since the exotic Vesta Beef Curries from the 1970s, which had to be presented with a ring of rice with the curry inside, just like the picture on the packet. They'd barely register on the spice scale. Indian restaurants seem to be everywhere so it's very easy to get that home delivery or pop in for a take-away: that's proper Anglo-Indian food!

Food	1st Choice	2nd Choice	3rd Choice
Balti	Cobra Beer	Wheat Beer	Hearty Rosé (e.g. Spanish, Portuguese)
Korma	Wheat Beer	Cobra Beer	Gin & Tonic
Rogan Josh	Wheat Beer	Hearty Rosé (e.g. Spanish, Portuguese)	IPA
Chicken Jalfrezi	Wheat Beer	IPA	Orange Wine
Chicken Tikka Masala	Cobra Beer	Wheat Beer	Hearty Rosé (e.g. Spanish, Portuguese)
Chicken Vindaloo	Perry	Nero d'Avola Rosé	Californian Pinot Noir
Madras	Wheat Beer	Chardonnay/Viognier Blend	Cobra Beer
Vindaloo	Perry	Hearty Rosé	Unoaked Pinot Noir

Sean from the Taste Team says:

Don't serve a Wheat Beer too cold or you'll lose the flavour: 8-12°C is best.

ITALIAN

"A bottle of red. A bottle of white.
Whatever kind of mood you're in tonight.
I'll meet you anytime you want in our
Italian Restaurant." Billy Joel

The Food: characterized by simple regional recipes using fresh, top quality ingredients
The Drink: red Chianti or white Vermentino

Could it be that pizza is now the most popular take-away dish? With so many companies offering home delivery it wouldn't be a surprise. Yet pizza is easy to make at home too. Italian cuisine is more than pizza and pasta. Each Italian region has its specialities. Some of these have become so international; we've forgotten where they come from.

Food	1st Choice	2nd Choice	3rd Choice
Arabbiata Sauce	Bardolino	Belgian Golden Ale	Sangiovese
Bolognese Sauce	Chianti Classico	Sangiovese	Bardolino
Carbonara Sauce (with Cream)	Vermentino	Sangiovese	Chianti Classico
Chicken Milanese	White Rioja	Vermentino	Italian Beer
Mushroom Ravioli	Vermentino	White Rioja	Fruity Rosé
Pesto Sauce	Chianti Classico	White Rioja	Bardolino
Pizza Margherita	Bardolino	Chianti Classico	Italian Beer
Tomato & Mozzarella Salad	Torrentés	Riesling	Fruity Rosé

Jilly from the Taste Team says:

Bardolino is quaffable, affordable and food friendly: great for midweek. But come the weekend, if your lasagne is luxurious, pick a good Chianti.

THAI

Thai cuisine is essentially a marriage of centuries-old Eastern and Western influences harmoniously combined into something uniquely Thai. - Thaigrocer.com

The Food: fresh, fragrant and flavoursome; can be eye-wateringly spicy.
The Drink: perry by far. Reds didn't figure at all.

Thai food is characterised by highly aromatic ingredients with spice. It's a complex cuisine with layers of flavours. The drink that complemented each and every dish and the unanimous winner was a basic perry.

Food	1st Choice	2nd Choice	3rd Choice
Satay	Perry	Singha Lager	Prosecco
Green Thai Curry	Perry	Gewurztraminer	Sancerre
Pad Thai	Perry	Gewurztraminer	Sancerre
Red Thai Curry	Perry	Prosecco	Fruity Rosé

Arti from the Taste Team says:

A little sweetness and fruit counteracts spice and heat.

TEA TIME
&
PUDS

TEA TIME & PUDS

We seem to have got out of the habit of having tea time, particularly a high tea. I recall Sundays in particular, after a blow-out roast lunch, nobody wanted much to eat later in the day. A couple of dainty sandwiches (triangles and crusts off as it was Sunday), and some sweet treats was all that was required. The Forsyte Saga always seemed to be on in the background!

Desserts are going the same way. With the sugar police around every corner, dare we even have a pud? If they're relegated to a treat at the weekend, does that make something sweet a thing to aspire to? Is that a good message?

My Gran used to say "A little of what you fancy does you good." We're much more inactive than she was back in the day. So maybe it's dessert, then take the dog for a walk.

If you fancy a proper high tea, consult the Sarnies pages under the British Snacks and Lunches section.

Long live Tea Time and the Pud!

CAKES & TEA TIME

Dost thou think, because thou art virtuous, there shall be no more cakes and ale?
William Shakespeare, Twelfth Night

The Food: sponge, pastry, fruit, icing: they can all be found in cakes.
The Drink: an overall crowd pleaser is Moscato d'Asti, a light, refreshing sparkling wine from Italy.

Cake, gâteau, kuche, torta – a little slice of sweetness mid afternoon to give that energy boost until dinner. We didn't taste test our cakes with cups of tea – maybe next time - rather we tried dessert wines, fortified wines and ales. For high tea, check the Sarnies section too. For carrot cake and mince pies, out of the drinks we tried, the beer came top. If you don't have beer, then try a dessert wine.

Food	1st Choice	2nd Choice	3rd Choice
Bakewell Tart	Moscato d'Asti	Ice Wine	Late Harvest Riesling
Banana Cake	Moscato d'Asti	Ice Wine	Monbazillac with Vanilla (blend of Sémillon, Muscadelle, Sauvignon Blanc)
Carrot Cake	IPA bitter	Moscato d'Asti	Beaumes de Venise dessert wine
Chocolate Cake	Sweet Sherry	Tawny Port	Liqueur Muscat
Fruit Cake	Sweet Sherry	Liqueur Muscat	Banyuls Dessert Wine
Ginger Cake	IPA bitter	Asti	Sweet Sherry
Mince Pie	Porter ale	Banyuls Dessert Wine	Cider
Scones, Cream & Jam	Moscato d'Asti	Ice Wine	Monbazillac

Maria from the Taste Team says:

Moscato d'Asti is so food friendly, particularly for sweet things. At around 7% ABV, it's light and refreshing too.

ICE CREAM

I Scream, You Scream, We All Scream for Ice Cream. - Song by Howard Johnson, Billy Moll, and Robert King, 1927

The Food: iced cream or juice with flavourings of fruit or spices. Can contain extra lumpy bits
The Drink: no overall winner: see below

Ice Cream is a refreshing dessert. I love using my ice cream maker and I have to boast that my cooked lemon ice cream and my strawberry ice cream are both rather popular. But regrettably neither is in Britain's Top 10! Strawberry ice cream can be overly sweet and cloying but with a dash of balsamic vinegar added to the fruit before you start, then it becomes fresh with a true strawberry zing.

Ice Cream	1st Choice	2nd Choice	3rd Choice
Butterscotch	Fruit Beer	Liqueur Muscat Dessert Wine	Barley Wine
Chocolate	Ruby Port	Stout	Liqueur Muscat Dessert Wine
Chocolate Chip Cookie Dough	Stout	Barley Wine	Ice Wine
Coconut	Moscato d'Asti	Tawny Port	Monbazillac
Cookies & Cream	Monbazillac	Ice Wine	Barley Wine
Mint Choc Chip	Australian Shiraz	Moscato d'Asti	Ice Wine
Raspberry Ripple	Ruby Port	Ice Wine	Monbazillac
Rocky Road	Ruby Port	Imperial Stout	Monbazillac
Salted Caramel	Tawny Port	Sweet Sherry	Stout
Vanilla	Monbazillac with Vanilla	Fruit Beer	Tawny Port

Jilly from the Taste Team says:

Add your drink to the ice cream. Cherries in Brandy over Vanilla! Bliss.

PUDS & DESSERTS

If you don't eat yer meat, you can't have any pudding. How can you have any pudding if you don't eat yer meat?
Another Brick in the Wall, Part II
Pink Floyd

The Food: a sweet dish following the main course Perry by far. Reds didn't figure at all.
The Drink: moscato d'Asti is a good all rounder for lighter desserts; maybe a Sweet Sherry for big puds.

We tested some good old-fashioned favourites with dessert wines, fortified wines and ales. Moscato d'Asti, a light, sparkling wine from Italy, is a good general pairing: it's low in alcohol and will be refreshing. If you prefer a slump on the sofa after your dessert, then a fortified wine or dessert wine will hit the spot.

Dessert	1st Choice	2nd Choice	3rd Choice
Apple & Blackberry Pie	Cider	Sweet Sherry	Liqueur Muscat Dessert Wine
Bread & Butter Pudding	Moscato d'Asti	Ice Wine	Monbazillac
Chocolate Pots	Banyuls	Liqueur Muscat	Tawny Port
Christmas Pud	Sweet Sherry	Porter	Banyuls Dessert Wine
Jam Roly Poly	Sweet Sherry	Moscato d'Asti	Tawny Port
Lemon Tart	Monbazillac	Moscato d'Asti	Beaumes de Venise
Steamed Pud	Banyuls	Tawny Port	Cider
Trifle	Moscato d'Asti	Ice Wine	Monbazillac

Arti from the Taste Team says:
Fit the weight of the food to the body of the wine. A heavy Christmas Pud will match well with the fortified sweet sherry.

HOW TO TASTE & PAIR

HOW TO TASTE & PAIR

In this section I've gathered together some more information about tasting. If I've used any jargon you don't understand, just check the glossary at the back of the book.

GLASSES

In the wine trade, professionals use a specially designed glass. The ISO tasting glass has a rounded bowl with a slightly tapered top and it holds 21.5cl. The narrower top allows you to get a full blast of the wine's aromas when you sniff.

The most important thing is that the wine glass has a stem. This is so that you don't warm up the wine by holding the bowl itself (don't copy actors in those American films). Also, you won't get greasy finger marks on the glass, which detracts from a wine's appearance.

Holding the foot of the glass allows you to swirl your wine like a pro. This can look quite pretentious but practice makes perfect. With a tasting sample in your glass (30-50ml), hold the foot of the glass and move in an anti-clockwise direction. If you're left handed, swirl in a clockwise direction.

The liquid should travel up the side of the glass and move around too. This aerates the wine allowing the aromas to come out. Don't do this with a full glass or your white shirt won't be white for very long. Don't have time for that nonsense? Keep your glass on the table and move in a circle.

Sparkling wines are usually served in a flute: a tall thin glass on a stem. Current thinking is that the wine is better in a normal wine glass as the aromas last longer and the wine is shown off to its best advantage.

There are special glasses for each type of wine or grape variety. You'd need a lot of storage to have a complete range let alone the mortgage to buy them all. I'd recommend you use what you've got. If your favourite wine tastes better at the pub or in a restaurant, then buy that style of glass for home.

Generally, for drinking during a meal, a larger style glass is kinder to a wine and will show it at its best rather than emphasise its faults. Look for a large tulip shape – a slight tapering at the top to concentrate the aromas. The knobbly crystal glasses passed down through the family have their place but maybe not for a mega-tasting: it could all end in tears.

For most beers, lagers, ciders or perries, the standard pint or half-pint glass is plenty good enough. If your ale should have a head, make sure it does, as this will help the aromas come out. The standard pint glass is easy to stack too. Purists might recommend different shapes for different styles but, again, you'll need a lot of storage space.

WHAT'S IN YOUR BOTTLE OF WINE:

I promote independent vintners wherever I can: they really do go that extra mile. Corks Out analysed what's in your bottle a couple of years ago and it still makes fascinating reading.

If you spend £4.99 on a bottle of wine, you're purchasing just 16p of wine quality. The rest of your money goes on tax (duty and VAT), margin, labour and shipping. As the price of a bottle increases, more of your money goes towards the wine quality, which has to be a good thing

If you spend £19.99 on a bottle of wine, your wine quality is £8.36, that's 52 times the wine quality for 4 times the price. I'm not suggesting you spend nearly twenty quid on your wine. I just want to point out that, we all like a bargain but, as with most things in life, you get what you pay for.

My advice is to spend a little bit more even if it means drinking a little less. Price quality ratio is important. Less insecticide, fewer sulphites: because I'm worth it.

TEMPERATURE

Temperature plays an important part in the taste of your drink. For whites and rosé wines, too cold and you won't be able to smell the aromas and your taste buds will be numbed. Room temperature for reds doesn't mean centrally-heated room temperatures in winter or placed in a sunny spot in summer. If the wine is too warm, the alcohol will tend to dominate and unbalance the wine. Here's a rough guide:

Drinks	Rough Temperature
Sparkling wines (low to high quality)	5-9°C
Sweet wines (low to high quality)	5-12°C
Rosé	6°C
Lager, wheat beers	6-8°C
Young white wines	8°C
Full-bodied, oaked whites	10°C
Light reds	12°C
Cider, Perry, IPA, Pale Ales and Bitters	12-14°C
Porters and Stouts	14°C
Tawny Port	15°C (but can be chilled too)
Sherry	17°C
Reds and Vintage Port	18°C

Before you change the temperature of your fridge, remember that just pouring the drink into a glass will add about 2°C to the starting temperature. Leading on from this, I don't fill a glass to the brim because it will have warmed up too much by the time I reach the bottom.

You can, of course, buy a wine thermometer if you want to be accurate. Indeed, you might already have one: tucked away in that drawer full of unused Christmas presents. For me, at home, life's a bit too short for that sort of malarkey, but there are a lot of people who like such accuracy. Your choice.

As a rule of thumb, the lighter the beer, the colder you serve it; the darker, the warmer you can drink it. The sweeter the cider, the colder it should be. If you want to disguise a poor wine, chill it – a LOT!.

BOTTLE CLOSURES

Most bottled beers have crown caps. Bottles of wine can have a real cork, a composite cork, an artificial cork or a screw cap. Sparkling wines and some ciders and specialist beers have a cork with a cage.

Screw caps, made of aluminium, have been looked down upon since they appeared on the market. Technology has moved on though and there are now different grades of screw cap, which do allow the wine to age nicely, just like a cork. On a picnic, or for speed at parties, it's hard to beat a screw cap.

Some wine regions wouldn't use anything but real corks. If there's a sense of occasion, a bottle with a cork adds to that sense of ritual. It's still the closure of choice for top wines, particularly if you want to keep them for the future. Cork is a natural product, coming from the cork oak tree Quercus suber (for those bottles you can't get the cork out of, maybe that should be Quercus sober).

Production techniques of corks have improved reducing the number of corked bottles of wine – you'll know if you've got one: a smell of musty carpets or damp cardboard.

Composite corks have a thin sliver of cork on the outside and man-made material on the inside. Artificial corks are made of plastic. These two types seem to mess with my bottle opener so I try to avoid them if I can but it's not always evident. Whilst they eliminate the risk of cork taint, they are rarely synonymous with quality wines.

With sparkling wines, I'd just like to add a word of caution. Undo the tin or aluminium foil, untwist the cage keeping your hand over the cork. Hold the bottle at an angle of about 45°, twist the bottle to release the cork. Be careful where you point the bottle, you could have someone's eye out – literally.

TO DECANT OR NOT?

The image of the crusty old gent with a decanter of aged wine at his elbow should stay just that: an image.

Decanting such a wine through a muslin or coffee filter will remove any sediment (making pouring and drinking cleaner, especially for vintage port), but it can unfortunately also remove some fruit aroma and taste.

Better to decant young, tannic wines with a highish alcohol content: the aeration will open up the wine. A good hour makes all the difference.

Just removing the cork and allowing the bottle to stand for a couple of hours will not aerate the wine. The surface area of the wine exposed to air is too small, as the only exposed part is in the neck of the bottle.

If you don't have a decanter, then pour the wine into a jug and then pour it back into the bottle before serving.

If you're not in charge of the bottle, and someone else has poured you a glass of wine, swirl, swirl and swirl again until you're happy with the aromas.

You can of course use a decanter for that BOGOF wine you got at the supermarket, which you don't want your guests to know you're serving.

BEFORE TASTING

Get yourself in the groove. This will be a learning experience: if only that you don't like a particular wine, beer or whatever you're tasting.

If you're going to a wine club or an organised tasting, in order to give your taste buds a chance, avoid these before drinking:

- Brushing your teeth
- Drinking coffee
- Chewing gum
- Hairspray or perfume
- Smoking
- Smelly environment
- Strong foods (spicy, minty, garlic, etc.)

If you've got a cold, whilst your friends might love to see you, don't waste your time by going to a tasting. You won't be able to catch the aromas nor the taste. Your friends won't want your germs either!

If there's a choice of wines, taste them in a logical order: light whites through to fortified wines; lower alcohol to higher alcohol. If you taste a complex Bordeaux Blend before a Vinho Verde, the subtlety of the white wine will be lost. With beers, take the hop content into account: high hops and alcohol should be tasted last.

Then again, you might not be tasting a dozen samples. Maybe you've got a few friends around to try different wines on a theme (Island Wines, New World vs Old World grape varieties, Italian whites, Global Riesling, for example). Or maybe you want to find out if you prefer beer, wine or a cup of tea with your beans on toast.

POURING FIZZY DRINKS

For beer, take a clean glass and angle it at 45°. Pour the beer from the bottle: a head is good as this allows you to smell the aromas. When the glass is about half full, gently bring the glass upright and keep pouring until the glass is full. If you're sampling a bottle-conditioned beer, watch out for the yeasts at the bottom of the bottle. If you like them, keep pouring but they will affect the brightness of the liquid. If you don't like them (apparently they give you rather windy after effects), stop pouring before they reach the glass.

For sparkling wines, ciders, perries, etc. use a similar technique.

TASTING YOUR DRINK

There are different types of tasting:

- Having a bottle in front of you: this enables you to identify what you're tasting with the information from the label.
- Comparisons: having two different drinks to compare and contrast
- Blind tasting: the most important aspect is to try to describe and define the wine rather than guessing the grape variety, vintage and country of origin. The latter is a bit of fun though – particularly if you get it right.

Pour a small measure into your glass (about 50ml). You might find this easier with 2 drinks to compare. Look at the contents of the glass (easier with a sheet of white paper behind/below):

- What colour is it?
- Is it clear and bright? Does it look as it should?
- Are there any bubbles?
- Is there a different colour at the rim?

Swirl your glass – you might find it easier to keep the glass on your table and move in a circle. The liquid should travel up the side of the glass. This aerates your drink allowing the aromas to come out. Don't do this with a full glass or you'll slosh all over yourself or a neighbour. You might notice "legs": this tells you how viscous the drink is.

Before the liquid settles again, smell it. Close your eyes if it helps. What can you smell?

- Floral?
- Fruits?
- Herbs and spices?
- Earthy notes (leaves, compost, soil)?
- Oak and smoke?

If you can smell several categories, then the drink is more complex and probably of a higher quality. How intense is the aroma? Do you recognise the smell – have you tasted this drink before?

Then take a sip of the drink. This will prepare your mouth for the second sip and cleanse it from previous sensations. Take a second sip.

Swirl the liquid around your mouth and tongue. You'll get the sensation of sweet, sour, salty (or mineral), bitter and umami (that elusive fifth element that is pleasantly savoury).

You might have seen or even heard wine professionals make noises at this point. They're drawing in some air through the liquid to aerate it in order to bring out the characteristics of what they're tasting. Think about the following questions:

- Are there any bubbles?
- Is the drink light, medium or full-bodied?
- Once you've swallowed (or used a spittoon), for how long does the taste linger in your mouth?
- Is the drink smooth in your mouth?
- Does your mouth dry up?
- Is the drink balanced? Or do some aspects, e.g. acidity, tannins, monopolise others.

CONCLUSIONS

What can you conclude from answering all those questions?

- The more aromas you catch, the more complex the drink and probably the finer it is
- Colour: a greenish yellow white wine is more than likely a young wine; whereas a golden yellow one is more likely older or oaked. With reds, a brick colour around the edge of the liquid would indicate some ageing.
- Colour might also indicate the ripeness of the grapes when they were harvested

- Carbon dioxide bubbles enhance the aromas and taste
- The mouth feel can determine the weight of the wine, sweetness, tannins, acidity, minerality, and alcohol levels
- Persistence in the mouth is often a sign of quality

TASTING FOOD

Put some food into your mouth. Chew it but don't swallow for a moment or two. Ask yourself these questions:
- Can you detect sweetness?
- Is it sugary sweet or just a hint of sweetness?
- How salty is the food?
- Is there any bitterness (e.g. smoked foods, charred BBQ meats, herbs)
- Is there any acidity in the food?
- How spicy is it?
- Does the food make you salivate or is it drying in your mouth?

Once you've swallowed:
- How long do the flavours linger in your mouth?
- What's the most dominant taste?
- Is the food lightweight, medium or heavyweight?

FOOD & DRINK PAIRING

You could argue that the best pairing for food is water and certainly we should be drinking lots of it according to the experts. I do tend to have a glass of water alongside my wine. With a mouthful of roast lamb and mint sauce, no wine is going to enhance that taste. Take a sip of water instead and move on to the next mouthful.

If you're out and about then make use of the sommelier. They are the link between the chef's creativity on the menu and the drinks on offer. At home though, use the recommendations in this book or keep notes of your own pairings.

To identify a harmonious match, take a sip of your drink. Take a bite of food and swallow. Take another bite of food and, before you swallow, take a sip of drink. I know this is the exact opposite of what your mother taught you but it's the best way to see if you've got that wow factor. This epitomises the cliché of the sum of the parts being greater than the individual components.

You'll know when you get it right for your taste. Some say this is better than sex. I couldn't possibly comment except to say that, once you know which food to match with which drink, you can have it wherever and whenever you choose.

Some tips to start you off on your own journey:

- We feast with our eyes first and we often subconsciously match colours, hence white wine with a white sauce, red wine with a red meat. Whilst this is a rule of thumb, there are many, many exceptions.
- Match the body, e.g. light delicate food with a light-bodied wine; robust tastes with a heavyweight drink.
- If the taste of the food lingers in the mouth, match with a drink that has similar persistence.
- If you're eating something moderately spiced, smoked, charred (e.g. BBQ), very herby, then opt for a smooth, fruity, even-off dry drink.
- Fiery hot, spicy food and some condiments (horseradish relish, mustard, wasabi, etc.) will overpower any drink so don't waste your best bottle.
- Meals that have a lot of liquid (stews, etc), and food that makes you salivate, can take a tannic wine. The food counteracts the drying nature of the tannins. This is the time to get out your Barolo or Malbec.

- Dishes that have a slight sweetness (potatoes, fish, seafood, dairy) will complement acidic drinks and even sparkling drinks.
- Bubbles can prolong the taste in your mouth as well as cleanse your palate.
- Match your drink to the strongest flavour on the plate.
- If you're still stuck, choose a drink that is local to the dish you're serving.

DRINKING IN GENERAL

Whilst I have a very positive attitude to drinks and feel there are great benefits, there is always a downside.

- Drinking makes you put on weight – if you've ever done Detox January, you'll have noticed this I'm sure. Who wants the six-pack of a Michelin man?
- Binge drinking is seriously bad for you and you'll probably eat more too
- Drink water alongside your alcoholic drink, or alternate between alcohol and a soft drink
- Have a few days off from alcohol each week
- Don't drink and drive: it's illegal and dangerous
- Don't mix alcohol with medication

In moderation, alcohol can stop you rusting, enrich mealtimes, be relaxing, and enhance social occasions. As the old'ns used to say: A little of what you fancy does you good.

STORING YOUR WINE

For unopened and opened drinks, think cool and dark. If you've got a lot of wine left over in the bottle, shove the cork back in and keep it in the fridge. Your wine will keep for a couple of days but remember to allow the wine to come back to the right temperature before finishing off.

Having tried all sorts of wine savers, I've found 'winesave' to be the best. It squirts argon gas into the bottle which, as argon is heavier than air, forms a blanket on top of the wine to stop it oxidising and losing its flavour. Stick the cork back in and keep cool and in the dark.

For sparkling drinks, sticking a teaspoon in the bottle is nonsense. There are tightly fitting caps you can use but they don't work for very long. Aim to consume the bottle within a few hours or a day. Failing that, use the blanket of 'winesave''s argon gas.

EXPERIMENTING AT HOME

If you don't really know what sort of wine you like, experimenting at home can be a great social and fun get-together.

The easiest way to do this is to buy a Taste Lab Kit from Honest Grapes Ltd. See Further Info towards the end of the book. You receive 5 test-tubes of different wines (there's a white wine pack and a red wine pack). By sipping the different anonymous wines and answering questions, you can determine your wine profile and from there, the grape varieties you're more likely to enjoy (and indeed those you don't like).

If there's a group of you though, it might be fun to try each of the following grape varieties, comparing and contrasting for the whites:

- Chardonnay
- Sauvignon Blanc
- Viognier
- Riesling
- Pinot Gris/Pinot Grigio

For the reds:
- Cabernet Sauvignon
- Merlot
- Shiraz
- Pinot Noir
- Tempranillo (Rioja)

Try to include one oaked bottle in these comparisons to find out if you like it oaky or not.

You may well end up with New World wines because the labels are in English. If you choose an independent retailer, they'll be able to help you pick some Old World wines for the mix.

For beers and ciders, compare and contrast two or three bottles. Lagers vs IPA vs Stout. Then compare the same style from different brands. You'll soon find your beer palate.

WHAT NEXT?

You might be lucky enough to have a wine tasting club or association within walking distance. Check on line.

For beers and ales, the pub is a good starting point. Some pioneering hostelries even offer tasting menus with matching beer flights.

For a treat, you could go to a gin tasting or maybe even design your own.

Maybe you'd like to host tastings with friends and family.

Everything is out there, but whatever you do, enjoy it.

AND FINALLY ....

From having fun at home, to special tasting menus with wine or beer, I hope I've spurred you on to rediscover what's on your plate and what to drink with it.

I'm just a regular, down-to-earth girl who's developed a passion for matching food and drink. To paraphrase the phenomenal Janet Webb: I'd like to thank all of you for reading my little book. If you've enjoyed it, then it's all been worthwhile.

Do let me know how you get on. I'm on Facebook and Twitter. I'll be updating results and listing new pairings so please like Quaffing & Scoffing and follow @Quaff_n_Scoff. Please join in.

Bottoms Up!

THE DRINKS PAGES

In this section you'll find the drinks we tested. I've described them and listed how they fared in our tests. I've also made some suggestions of other food pairings.

If you've got a particular drink in mind, this section might give you inspiration for matching a particular dish.

Dip in and out and have fun discovering what else you can try.

The alcohol by volume (ABV) measurements are given as a percentage.

Chin Chin!

BANYULS APPELLATION

Characteristics

Juicy red fruit (especially strawberries), prunes and sweet spices. Hot summers and constant on-shore winds made the vines' life difficult. The yields are low and harvesting is long and slow: hand picking on steep, coastal slopes. The grapes are often part shrivelled, intensifying the complex character of the wine. Beautifully balanced, more port-like than a full dessert wine.

Grape:	Fortified Grenache (Grenache Noir, less often Grenache Gris or Grenache Blanc) with a mix of Muscat, Mourvèdre, Carignan, Macabeu and Tourbat grape varieties producing a fortified dessert wine
Origins:	Banyuls-sur-Mer on the French Mediterranean coast in the region of Roussillon, close to the Spanish border.
Acidity:	Low-medium
Body:	Full
Tannins:	Medium
Oak:	Yes
ABV:	About 15 - 16%

Food Pairing:

Winner: in our tastings, Banyuls came 1st with steamed treacle pudding and joint first with mince pies. It's an infamous pairing with chocolate. Try drinking as an apéritif too.

Loser: Light dishes

Nick from the Taste Team says:
If you like a young, fruity port, give a Banyuls a try.

BARDOLINO APPELLATION

Characteristics

This is a simple, crowd pleasing red wine yet it's very food friendly. Fruity, particularly sour cherries, fresh and herby, it's light, smooth and usually well balanced. You can chill this uncomplicated wine if you wish. The Bardolino Superiore DOCG is aged before release and is a little more complex.

Grape:	A blend of principally Corvina with Rondinella and small amounts of Molinara and other authorised grape varieties.
Origins:	Named after the town on the shores of Lake Garda, in the Veneto region in NE Italy with both DOC and DOCG wines.
Acidity:	Medium
Body:	Light
Tannins:	Low-Medium
ABV:	10.5 - 11.5%

Food Pairing

Winner: Bardolino came:

- 1st in our pizza tasting, Pasta and Arabbiata Sauce, Steak and Mushroom Pie and Toad in the Hole.
- 3rd with Shepherd's Pie and = 3rd with Cottage Pie.
- This wine will also match pork, veal, meaty fish (tuna, swordfish), chicken and turkey.

Loser: Hearty fare will overpower the wine.

Jilly from the Taste Team says:

A super, modest, quaffable food-friendly wine. Always keep a couple handy for emergencies.

BAROLO APPELLATION

Characteristics

Before it's released to the market, a basic Barolo has to be at least 38 months old, 18 of which must be in wood. The Riserva category must be at least 62 months old.

Known as The King of Wines – perhaps in competition to its neighbouring DOCG Barbaresco (also made from Nebbiolo) - Barolo is surprisingly light in colour. Its characteristics include aromas of rose petals, tar, herbs, liquorice, truffles and chocolate. It ages very well and a sommelier friend of mine won't open a bottle if it's less than 10 years old.

There is a modern trend to make Nebbiolo more approachable, designing a wine that is fruit forward, earlier drinking, unoaked or less oaked. This sort of wine won't display the coveted DOCG of Barolo.

Grape:	Nebbiolo
Origins:	Now an up-market DOCG, this dry wine was named in honour of the Marchesa de Barolo in 1850s (before then the wine was very sweet and fruity – a completely different style).
Grown:	Piedmont in Italy
Acidity:	Medium-High
Body:	Med-Full
Tannins:	Med-High
Oak:	Yes – although you might find more modern styles without .
ABV:	About 13-16%

Food Pairing

Winner: Our basic Barolo was 1st for Roast Duck. We reckon it would be top for Roast Goose too. Test it yourself if you're celebrating Michaelmas. It'll need a good gravy or jus to soften the tannins.

Loser: Light and delicate dishes would be lost with Barolo, which is very intense.

Penny from the Taste Team says:

When ready to drink, this wine has an elegance that is just divine.

BEAUJOLAIS VILLAGES APPELLATION

Characteristics

Light and fruity, this wine is refreshing (especially when chilled) and quaffable with a little spice to make it interesting. You'll get strawberries and cherries on the nose and a fresh finish. Drink it young: within 2 years of harvest.

If you want a more robust Beaujolais, then choose a wine from one of the Beaujolais crus, which will contain the village name:

- Brouilly, Chiroubles, Regnié, (the lightest);
- Côte de Brouilly, Fleurie, St Amour (medium-bodied wines);
- Chénas, Julienas, Morgan, Moulin à Vent (these wines are designed to be drunk around 5 years after harvest).

Grape:	Gamay producing a light red wine
Origins:	The Romans introduced wine making to the Beaujolais area in France, the southern-most part of Burgundy. The Beaujolais Villages appellation consists of elevated vineyards and considered superior to a basic Beaujolais. It makes up around 15% of total Beaujolais production.
Acidity:	Medium-High
Body:	Light
Tannins:	Low
ABV:	About 12.5%

Food Pairing

Winner: Tuna steak, ham, lunchtime light dishes, picnics

Loser: Robust stews and heavyweight dishes would overpower this wine, unless you're tasting an aged Cru.

Penny from the Taste Team says:

If you open a bottle and don't like it, add orange slices, white rum (spiced is good too), sugar and some orange juice and, hey, you've got Sangria.

BORDEAUX BLEND

Characteristics

Cabernet Sauvignon and Merlot are the main components in a Bordeaux Blend, with one or more of the other grape varieties included in small quantities. These wines are made for ageing and in a great vintage they'll last for decades – with an appropriate price tag! Most supermarkets will stock an entry-level version.

There's no official designation of a Bordeaux Blend. In fact, you might see "claret" on the labels of bottles aimed at the British market. Claret is the word the English used back in the 1700s to describe wine from Bordeaux. Some wine makers are experimenting with the addition of Sangiovese and other grape varieties. Time will tell ....

You'll find blackcurrant, black cherry and plum, vanilla, spice, liquorice and maybe a whiff of coffee. There'll be a big structure and persistent flavours. When young, these wines can be austere. If you've opened one and it's not to your taste: decant it and leave for a little while.

Grape:	A blend from two or more of Cabernet Sauvignon, Cabernet Franc, Carmenère, Malbec, Merlot, Petit Verdot, producing a complex, red wine
Origins:	France
Grown:	Bordeaux, Italy (Super Tuscans), USA (Called Meritage), Australia, Chile, Argentina, and South Africa
Acidity:	Medium-High
Body:	Medium-Full
Tannins:	High
Oak:	Yes
ABV:	13-14%

Food Pairing

Winner: a basic Bordeaux Blend came 1st with Roast Lamb and 2nd with Roast Beef.

Loser: Simple, delicate foods, fish dishes, salads.

Francis from the Taste Team says:

It's hard to beat a good claret. These wines will have a long finish in the mouth – make sure your food does too.

CABERNET SAUVIGNON

Characteristics

You can smell blackcurrant, green bell pepper, eucalyptus, cedar, tobacco, spices. Its colour is very dark, especially when young, it has a distinctive smell of blackcurrants and, if barrel aged, cedar and even tobacco too. If the grapes are not fully ripe, there will be herbaceous or green pepper tones.

Cabernet Sauvignon is an important component in Bordeaux Blends, where blending can compensate for climatic influences. It's blended with one or more of Merlot, Cabernet Franc, Malbec, Carmenère, Petit Verdot, and, outside of France, with Sangiovese or Syrah/Shiraz. You can find this grape as a single varietal wine too, particularly in warmer climates, as it is a late-budding and late-ripening grape variety.

Cabernet Sauvignon wines can be long lived. This is because the little grapes have thick skins, and the proportion of juice to all the other matter (fleshy bits, large pips, skin) is small so the wines have quite high tannins. Young wines can be harsh so look for more mature specimens. In warmer climes, the wines will be fruitier, maybe even jammy, and more alcoholic.

Cabernet Sauvignon works well with oak. The wood imparts a vanilla note to the wine, which adds complexity.

Grape:	Black grape making red wine
Origins:	Bordeaux, France
Grown	France, Chile, USA, Italy, Australia, South Africa, Spain, Germany, UK, Bulgaria, Czech Republic, Georgia, Hungary, Moldova, Romania, Slovenia, Ukraine, Cyprus, Greece, Israel, Lebanon, Argentina, Brazil, Peru, Uruguay, New Zealand, China: virtually everywhere is the wine world.
Relations	Offspring of Cabernet Franc and Sauvignon Blanc; parent of Marselan
Acidity:	Medium
Body:	Full
Oak	Frequent
Tannins:	High
ABV:	13.5-15.5%

Food Pairing

Winner: Prepare dishes which have a long length of flavour in the mouth to match the full-bodied, persistent wine: slow cooked dishes such as oxtail, stews, roast game and game casseroles; big lumps of lamb and herbs will go well, steak with sauces, Cheddar cheese, bitter dark chocolate. Full-bodied foods to go with the full-bodied wine.

A single varietal Cabernet Sauvignon came 3rd with Roast Lamb and a Burger. As part of a Bordeaux Blend, it came first with Roast Lamb, 2nd with Roast Beef.

Loser: Hot, spicy food as the spices will clash with the tannins. Light and delicate dishes will be overpowered by the wine.

Sean from the Taste Team says:

To really get to know this grape variety, taste test a single varietal bottle of wine together with some blends.

CHARDONNAY

Characteristics

From green apple, pear, to citrus to pineapple; crisp or buttery mouthfeel; vanilla if oaked. The winemaker and the terroir have a huge influence on Chardonnay characteristics.

Chardonnay is a green-skinned grape, making white wines, which can be still or sparkling (it is the essential ingredient for Champagne), oaked or buttery.

In cool climates, this grape variety makes crisp wines with fruit flavours of green apple and pear, with a light to medium body. Basic wines such as these will be relatively inexpensive.

In warmer regions, flavours tend to be more citrus, peach and melon leading to tropical fruits in very warm climates.

Malolactic fermentation softens the acidity and fruit flavours leaving a buttery sensation in the mouth and maybe some hazelnut tones.

Oaked Chardonnays bring vanilla, spice and even a little smoke to the mix. It's expensive to use oak barrels so expect to pay significantly more for these wines, but you will gain from the complexity, intensity, persistence in the mouth, and well-integrated oak flavours. These wines tend to be fuller bodied, ideal for that roast chicken.

Terroir will also affect the price: white Burgundies from France or wines from Russian River Valley in California, where the grape variety finds ideal growing conditions, attract a premium.

Still wines are usually 100% Chardonnay, but you might come across some blends too: Chardonnay with sémillon, Colombard, Viognier, or Sauvignon Blanc. Chardonnay will bring body to the wine as well as a roundness in the mouth and some persistence.

Grape:	Green grape making white wine (both still and sparkling)
Origins:	Burgundy, France
Grown:	France, USA, Australia, Italy, Spain, New Zealand, South Africa, Chile, Argentina, Hungary, Canada, Austria, Bulgaria, Greece, Israel, Lebanon, Germany, Georgia, Great Britain, Slovakia, Macedonia, Moldova, Portugal, Romania, Slovenia, Serbia, Switzerland: virtually every wine producing country.
Acidity:	Moderate Acidity
Body:	Light-medium
Tannins:	If oaked, light
Oak:	Often (check the back label)
ABV:	Mostly 12.5-14%

Food Pairing

Winner: Champagne/sparkling wine: seafood, fried fish, fried chicken, blinis and smoked salmon, light dishes

Young unoaked (e.g. basic Chablis): fish, seafood, canapés and light starters, it came:

- 1st for Chicken Caesar Salad, Ham Hock, Egg & Potato Salad, Jacket Potato with Cheese;
- 2nd for Rocket with Poached Salmon, Jacket Potato with Tuna & Sweetcorn and a plain green salad.
- An unoaked Australian Chardonnay came 1st for BBQ Chicken, BBQ Seafood Kebabs, Green Salad, Veggie Kebabs

- 2nd for BBQ Halloumi and BBQ Salmon.

Warm climate unoaked (e.g. New Zealand, South Africa, Chile): salmon, fish cakes, pasta in a creamy sauce. A very lightly oaked Chardonnay from Chile came:

- 1st for Fish Cakes;
- 2nd for Tuna & Sweetcorn Sarnie, Leek & Potato Soup, Mulligatawny Soup;
- 3rd for Prawn Mayo Sandwich, Smoked Salmon & Cream Cheese Sandwich, Minestrone soup, Mushroom soup.

An oaked more mature Chardonnay will match more complex foods, such as creamy chicken and ham pie, roast chicken and roast turkey, pumpkin ravioli, rich fish, Cheddar cheese. A lightly oaked Chardonnay came

- 1st for Salmon en Croûte;
- 2nd for Fish Pie, Roast Chicken and Salmon Fillet.

Grilled chicken, pork roast, veal, and lobster are the sorts of foods, which pair well with a Chardonnay that has undergone malolactic fermentation and has more complexity.

Loser: goats cheese, smoked fish and meats (don't oak and smoke), tomato-based dishes.

Jilly from the Taste Team says:
From the most exquisite, most expensive Burgundies to affordable mass-produced quaffable wines: there's a Chardonnay for everyone.

CHENIN BLANC

Characteristics

A honey note is the traditional aroma from cool climate Chenin Blanc wines, like the Loire in France. Always fruity, wherever it's grown.

Crémant de Loire is a tasty sparkling wine from France: great as an apéritif. Another Loire wine is Vouvray: this can also be sparkling and off-dry.

South Africa has appropriated Chenin Blanc and it is the most widely planted grape variety of any wine region in the world. Here you can find fresh and fruity wines to be drunk young; oaked wines; sweet, unctuous dessert wines and blends.

Grape:	Green grape making white wine (both still and sparkling, dry to sweet, and some fortified wines)
Origins:	The Loire, France
Relations:	Sauvignon Blanc, Colombard, Sauvignon
Grown:	South Africa, France, USA
Acidity:	High Acidity
Body:	Light-Full, depending on the style.
Oak:	Occasionally, check the label.
ABV:	Mostly 12-15%

Food Pairing

Winner: 1st with Fish Pie; 2nd Salade Niçoise and Roast Pork, 3rd Waldorf Salad.
Loser: Get the balance right so avoid robust foods.

Nick from the Taste Team says:

This is an under-rated wine. South African Chenins might be cheaper but I reckon the French have the edge on quality.

CHIANTI APPELLATION

Characteristics

Ruby red colour, red fruit, especially raspberries, violets, herbaceous, minerality, silky tannins and balanced acidity. You will find a lesser quality simple Chianti which comes from outside the Chianti Classico zone, but, within the zone, Chianti Classico is the most basic red.

Higher up in quality is Chianti Classico Riserva (oaked and aged before release) and higher again is the long-lived Chianti Classico Gran Selezione (more oak and age).

Chianti is particularly food friendly. A basic one for midweek and then a finer, more elegant and pricier one for the weekend. If you have a stash of wine, there should definitely be a Chianti in there.

Grape	At least 80% Sangiovese plus up to 20% of other authorised grape varieties, including Cabernet Sauvignon and Merlot.
Origins	Geographical region in Chianti, Tuscany, NW Italy. The Chianti Classico area is a regulated zone at the heart of Chianti and has been awarded the top DOCG (i.e. the quality should be better than a simple Chianti). We tasted a Chianti Classico DOCG.
Acidity	Medium to high
Body	Full
Oak	Frequently
Tannins	Medium
ABV	At least 12%

Food Pairing

Winner: Awarded:

- 1st for Pasta & Pesto as well as Spag Bol and Roast Ham;
- 2nd for Toad in the Hole, Roast Chicken Pie, Roast Pheasant and Steak & Mushroom Pie;
- =3rd for Cottage Pie;
- 3rd for Cumberland Pie and Roast Chicken Pie.
- Good too with a burger, Americans use lasagna, roasts, grilled meats, rabbit, BBQs. An excellent food friendly wine.

Loser: Delicate dishes will be lost with this wine.

Maria from the Taste Team says:

I don't know anyone who doesn't like this wine with food. It's one of my favourites and reminds me of when I lived near Tuscany.

CIDER

Characteristics

Cider can be clear, bright and sparkling through to dark, still and cloudy, sweet to dry. You might also find a single varietal cider, cider made by the Champagne method, and individual craft ciders.

Various aromas and flavours are expressed depending on the type of cider you're drinking, but always apples. We tested a bog-standard readily available medium-dry sparkling cider for our pairings.

Fruit:	Different varieties of cider apple fruit, some ciders include dessert or cooking apples too.
Origins:	Although apple orchards were planted during Roman times, documentary evidence of cider making comes after the Norman conquest.
Acidity:	Medium
Tannins:	Low to High
Body:	Light to medium
ABV:	1.2-8.5+%; our tests: 4.5%

Food Pairing

Winner: Cider came
- =1st for a Chip Butty, a Fish Finger Sandwich, as well as Mashed Potato on its own!
- 1st for Apple & Blackberry pie, Waldorf Salad, Burgers, Pork Chops and Burgers;
- 3rd for Bangers & Mash, Toad in the Hole, Roast Chicken, Roast Ham, Roast Pork and Fish & Chips.

We didn't test these but:

- if you're cooking with cider, drink it too;
- a medium cheddar will match the fruitiness of the cider and the bubbles will cleanse the palate;
- if you're using apples in the dish, cider should work too, e.g. pork and apple; pizza is also often recommended.

Loser: Chocolate, dishes with a tomato-based sauce, blue cheese.

Francis from the Taste Team says:

For a lunchtime drink, which will still allow you to get things done in the afternoon, cider's ideal.

CÔTES DU RHÔNE APPELLATION

Characteristics

You're most likely to find a Côtes du Rhône wine from the Southern Rhône, which will be dominated by Grenache in the blend. Influenced by the Mediterranean, the climate here is warmer and more stable leading to richer, brighter wines with more alcohol.

Grenache brings fruit, a little spice and alcohol; Syrah gives colour, structure and spice; and Mourvèdre offers colour, fruit, hint of chocolate and backbone.

A Côtes du Rhône wine from the Northern Rhône will be dominated by Syrah. The climate is cooler here so the wines will be a little more complex than those from further south.

Grape:	A core blend of Grenache, Syrah, Mourvèdre, (known as GSM) with a dash of up to 10 others to make red wine. You'll find a small quantity of white and rosé wines too
Origins:	The Rhône Valley is split into two wine regions: Northern Rhône and Southern Rhône. The Côtes du Rhône appellation is the most basic and uncomplicated of the regulated wines and comes from both north and south. This wine is a good starting point to experiment in the region.
Acidity:	Medium
Body:	Full
Oak	Usually
Tannins:	Medium
ABV:	13-14.5%

As Côtes du Rhône is the lowest classification, the rules aren't too strict so quality can be variable. Do your research or go up a level to Côtes du Rhône Villages, Côtes du Rhône Village (with a named village) or one of the village crus, e.g. Châteauneuf-du-pape.

Food Pairing

Winner: Côtes du Rhône came

- 1st for Sausages with Onion Gravy, and Roast Beef;
- 3rd with Roast Duck.
- Also pair with BBQs, goose, venison, stews, hearty winter fare.

Loser: This wine will overpower light dishes and most fish.

Sean from the Taste Team says:
If you like this wine, try too a GSM blend from Australia.

ENGLISH SPARKLING WINE

Characteristics

English Sparkling Wine's reputation is getting better and better thanks to the dedicated wine makers who aim for quality not quantity. Whilst not a cheap option, for special occasions and celebrations, it's a top-notch choice. Made in the Champagne method (second fermentation in the bottle), look for fine bubbles, which cleanse the palate, yeasty/brioche aromas and a fresh finish.

Just like Champagne, you'll find Blanc de Blancs wines (i.e. wines made exclusively from white wine grapes), Blanc de Noirs wines (i.e. a wine made from black grapes: Pinot Noir and/or Pinot Meunier) as well as blends from both white wine and red wine grapes. The dry Brut style is the most popular.

Many Sparkling Wine aficionados drink this style of wine in traditional wine glasses and not flûtes. The normal wine glasses will enhance the wine's aroma, but don't use girt big ones.

Grape:	A blend of one or more of Chardonnay, Pinot Noir and Pinot Meunier
Origins:	England: Christopher Merrett is deemed to have been Dom Perignon's forerunner by, in 1662, formally documenting the addition of sugar to make a sparkling wine. This, coupled with coal-fired production of stronger glass bottles in 17th Century, makes England the birthplace of this type of sparkling wine.
Acidity:	Medium-High
Body:	Medium
ABV:	12-13%

Food Pairing

Winner: We tested a Blanc de Noirs English Sparkling Wine and it came:

- 1st with Fish & Chips.
- Also great as an apéritif and with canapés. The acidity of the wine cuts through fried food and the bubbles cleanse the mouth ready for the next forkful.
- 2nd with Fried Chicken.

Loser: Whilst there's a style for most dishes, be careful to get the right one: a Demi-Sec or Doux with dessert or cheese will be much more pleasurable than a Brut.

Jilly from the Taste Team says:
Fish & Chips with an English Sparkling Wine: a perfect pairing

FRUIT JUICE

Characteristics

The liquid that results from squeezed or pressed fruits. May contain added water and/or sugar. Can be freshly squeezed or made up from concentrated juice. Fruit juices have been highlighted recently for containing too much sugar and not enough fibre. One answer is to dilute it with ice or water.

I've recently come across a watermelon juice drink, which was not too sweet, delicate but refreshing too.

Fruit:	Different varieties of fruits: e.g. orange, apple, pineapple, tomato, blends.
Origins:	As old as dirt but certainly known to prevent scurvy by 1400s (the Portuguese Vasco de Gama used it in his expeditions).
Acidity:	Medium to High
Body:	Light to medium

Food Pairing:

Winner: The acidic orange juice was a hit with a Bacon Butty and a Full English Breakfast. The acidity cuts through the fats and refreshes the mouth. Orange juice would also work as your soft drink at BBQs.

Watermelon Juice Drink went very well with both Fried Egg and Poached Egg. Both foods are quite delicate and complemented each other.

Loser: Milky foods and acidic foods: acid foods and acid drinks can lead to an unpleasant aftertaste.

GEWÜRTZTRAMINER

Characteristics

Gewürtztraminer (or Gewürtz to its fans) is an aromatic grape variety, which can be made into dry or sweet wine, and everything in between. Whichever style, the aroma of lychees is its signature. You'll find too grapefruit, rose, and, if the grapes were very ripe, pineapple.

That is the hard part: waiting until the grapes are ripe yet making wine with sufficient acidity for a well-balanced wine.

The sweet wines, e.g. Vendanges Tardives, use botrytised grapes (a naturally occurring fungus) and will have enhanced aromas including honey, sweet spices and even a whiff of smokiness.

By the way: the French don't put an umlaut in Gewürtz, but umlaut or not, it's the same grape variety.

Grape:	Pinky skinned grape making white wine.
Origins:	Most likely Germany
Grown:	France (notably Alsace), Germany, N Italy, Hungary, Romania, Croatia, Slovenia, New Zealand, Australia, USA, Canada, South Africa
Relations:	Mutation from Traminer (aka Savagnin Blanc).
Acidity:	Low
Body:	Medium
ABV:	11-16%

Food Pairing

Winner: The Gewürztraminer we tasted came:

- =1st with Green Thai Curry and Ginger Beef;
- 2nd with Green Thai Curry and Pad Thai.
- Try also with Münster Cheese or Stinking Bishop; terrines and pâtés.

Loser: Very light dishes would be overpowered by the aromatic wine.

Nick from the Taste Team says:

A versatile wine which you either love or hate.

GRENACHE / GARNACHA

Characteristics

Red berries (raspberries and strawberries), black cherry, herbaceous, sweet spices and white pepper spice, high alcohol, smooth. The light colour belies the bodyweight.

A mainstay of Châteauneuf-du-Pape, from the French Rhône Valley, this grape variety also forms up to 20% of Rioja wines from Spain.

See also Banyuls (for a dessert Grenache), Côtes du Rhône and Rioja.

Grape:	Black grape making red (blends and single varietal) and rosé wines, sweet or dry.
Origins:	Aragon, Spain where it's known as Garnacha.
Grown:	France, Spain, USA, Australia
Acidity:	Low-Medium
Body:	Full
Oak:	Frequent
Tannins:	Medium
ABV:	13.5-15%

Food Pairing

Winner: The basic IGP red from the Pays d'Oc, France that we tested came:

- 1st with Tomato Soup and =1st with Oxtail Soup;
- 2nd for a Ham & Mustard Sarnie and French Onion Soup;
- Try also with Sausages & Gravy, BBQs, stews and wholesome dishes.

We tasted a supermarket Garnacha rosé from Navarra in Spain: it was full of red fruits on the nose and palate with a rounded and balanced mouthfeel. Whilst it didn't come first with any of the Indian dishes we tried it with, it did come 3rd overall: so if you're looking for a consistent wine for your take-away, this would be a pretty good choice.

Loser: Avoid the red wine with light fish dishes and delicate foods.

Sean from the Taste Team says:

You'll often find Grenache as part of a GSM blend, along with Shiraz and Mourvèdre, especially from Australia.

GRÜNER VELTLINER

Characteristics

White pepper is the trade-mark spice of this wine, citrus, fresh and fruity. If you search hard, you'll find much more expensive bottle-aged wines which acquire a nuttiness and creaminess which adds to the complexity of the wine. These wines are generally higher in alcohol.

Grape	Green grape making a trendy white wine.
Origins	Random cross in Austria, where it is now the country's most important grape variety
Grown	Austria, Slovakia, Czech Republic, NE Italy, recent plantings in New Zealand, Australia, USA and Canada.
Relations	Offspring of Traminer (Savagnin in France) and St Georgen.
Acidity	High
Body	Medium
Oak	Occasionally
ABV	About 11-12.5%

Food Pairing

Winner: A young Grüner Veltliner came:

- 1st in our Pork Sausage tasting;
- 3rd with a Chip Butty and Chip Butty with Ketchup;
- It would also go with chicken, firm fish and veal (Wiener Schnitzel).

Loser: Heavyweight foodstuffs would overpower this wine.

Penny from the Taste Team says:

The acidity of the wine cuts through any fattiness to make a wonderful mouthful.

ICED TEA

Characteristics

A refreshing iced drink easily made at home. Early recipes for Regent's Punch (1811) required green tea with orange and lemon mixed with brandy, rum, arrack, pineapple juice and champagne. Knock out!

For the taste test, we used a basic commercial lemon iced tea, which is very common in supermarkets. The team felt it was overly sweet but the tannins and acidity show great potential for food pairing.

Origins:	The first recorded recipe comes from the late 1700s.
Relations:	Traditionally flavoured with citrus, but now syrups (peach, mango), other fruits and herbal teas are used. Try jasmine, chai, or oolong.
Acidity:	Medium
Body:	Medium
Tannins:	Medium

Food Pairing:

Winner: the tea came:

- 1st in our Coronation Chicken Sarnie tasting and showed consistent results throughout that Soups & Sarnies evening.
- Texturally, it worked well with moist sandwich fillings (Tuna & Sweetcorn and Egg & Cress) as succulence counteracts the tannins, and the acidity harmonizes with any sweetness.
- 2nd for Carrot & Coriander Soup.

Loser: sweet dishes will emphasise the drinks acidity.

Francis from the Taste Team says:

A great drink for any guests who are driving.

IPA (INDIAN PALE ALE)

Characteristics

The trademark of an English IPA is hops: medium to high hop aroma; medium to high hop flavour as well as hop's traditional bitterness. IPAs also have medium maltiness and body. This all makes a dry crisp beer with a colour ranging from pale gold to deep copper.

American IPAs will tend to be more floral and fruity, particularly citrus, due to different hops.

Imperial or Double IPA is a bigger beast altogether: fuller bodied, higher in alcohol, medium to high maltiness, deeper colour, intense hop.

Origins:	England: an export style of Pale Ale, which benefitted from the long voyage to India in the early 1800s.
Made:	England, Canada, USA, and craft breweries around the world.
IBU:	English IPA: 40-60; American IPA: 40-70; Imperial IPA: 60-120
Body:	Medium-Full
ABV:	From 4% to 8.8%

Food Pairing

Winner: The English IPA we tasted (at 5.6%) came:

- 1st with Carrot Cake and =1st with Ginger Cake. The spices in both cakes worked well with the IPA.
- 1st with BBQ sausages, Cheeseburger, Fried Chicken and Hot Dog;
- 2nd for Chicken Jalfrezi and Veggie Kebabs
- 3rd Rogan Josh.

Loser: Sweet, sweet dishes. Unfortunately, our traditional English dishes (Fish & Chips and Bangers & Mash) didn't fare well at all either.

Maria from the Taste Team says:

IPA and cake was a revelation. A tasty combination for high tea.

LAGER

Characteristics

In the UK, lager generally refers to a pale, carbonated beer, a sort of Pilsner style. In fact this type of lager is the most brewed and sold in the world.

Everyday lagers are usually light to mid golden in colour, mild in flavour yet hoppy, smooth and refreshing. It's very easy to drink especially in hot weather when it's chilled. As a rule of thumb, the lighter the colour, the colder it's served.

Indian-style lager: brewed in the UK to complement different food styles, particularly Indian foods. Less gassy than other lagers, the most popular lager is particularly smooth. Look out for the alcohol-free versions if you're driving.

Thailand too has a lager-style beer, which is rich and hoppy and quite full bodied. The carbonation refreshes and cleanses the palate between mouthfuls.

Origins:	Germany
Made:	Worldwide
Body:	Light to Medium
IBU:	30-45
ABV:	4%-6%

Food Pairing

Winner: The Indian Lager we tested came:

- 1st for Chicken Tikka Masala and Balti;
- Overall 2nd for our Indian Takeaway tasting;
- 3rd for Ham Hock, Egg & Potato Salad;

- Try lagers with seafood, mild cheese, salmon.

Loser: Full-flavoured dishes will overpower most everyday lagers.

Penny from the Taste Team says:

Lager means warehouse in German – so stock up!

MALBEC

Characteristics

Robust and dark red, Malbec is a powerful, hearty wine. It's one of the six varieties allowed in a claret, and still the core ingredient of Cahors wine, from SW France.

Yet its recent success belongs to Argentina, particularly in Mendoza. Malbec benefits from a long ripening season, which gives complexity and depth to its flavour. Cool climates produce more acidic, spicier, less fruit-forward wines. Warmer climes emphasise the fruit (plums, black cherries, blackberries), with leather and chocolate.

Grape:	Black grape making red wine.
Origins:	Bordeaux, France but now Argentina's signature grape
Grown:	Argentina, France, Italy, Chile, Australia, NZ, US, South Africa, Canada.
Acidity:	Low-Medium
Body:	Full
Tannins:	Medium-High
Oak:	Can be unoaked (drink young) or oaked (may be aged).
ABV:	13.5-15%

Food Pairing

Winner: Steak, big BBQs, stews, hearty fare. Malbec came 2nd for our BBQ ribs and BBQ Steak.

Loser: anything delicate will be overpowered by the wine

Francis from the Taste Team says:

Taste the food before you season: salt and pepper accentuate the alcohol.

MERLOT

Characteristics

Tasting of plum, raspberry, black cherry, red fruit, herbaceous, spice, soft, juicy mouthfeel, luscious. Merlot is one of the grape varieties in a Bordeaux Blend (see other recommendations under that title).

Merlot is a thin-skinned grape. For Bordeaux-style wines, it tends to be harvested early leading to a crisper, medium-bodied, moderately alcoholic wine with red fruit and herbaceous notes.

After being slated in the film Sideways, Merlot sales are recovering! The film was so influential that wine sales overall increased after the film's release.

New World styles from warmer climates tend to be fuller bodied, higher in alcohol, low acidity, with black fruit tones, the grape being harvested at full ripeness.

Grape:	Black grape for red wine.
Origins:	Bordeaux, France
Grown:	France, Italy, USA, Australia, Chile, Argentina, South Africa, Spain, NZ, Bulgaria
Relations:	Offspring of Cabernet Franc and the relatively unknown Madeleine Noire des Charentes; half-sibling of Cabernet Sauvignon
Acidity:	Low-Medium
Body:	Medium-Full
Tannins:	Low; smooth
Oak:	Frequent
ABV:	12-15%

Food Pairing

Winner: as a single varietal, Merlot came

- 2nd with Roast Ham;
- 3rd Roast Pheasant;
- Chicken, roast turkey, sausages, rabbit, Italian dishes (with tomato) would also work.

Loser: dishes with creamy sauces; light fish; leafy green veggies.

Penny from the Taste Team says:

The one word to describe this wine is smooooooooooth!

MILK

Characteristics

A pale liquid produced by the mammary glands of mammals. Milk is a fine source of calcium and amino acids, which are good for bones, teeth and the healthy function of your body. It also fills you up so you don't eat so much – result!

Cows milk is commonly supplied in bottles with a blue cap (full fat), green cap (semi-skimmed), red cap (skimmed). Because skimmed milk has less fat, it contains more protein by volume than full fat milk.

It's now reasonably common to find soya milk, almond milk and coconut milk in supermarkets too.

Origin:	Cows, goats, sheep
Made:	Worldwide
Relations:	Butter, cheese, cream, ice cream, yoghurt.
Acidity:	Low
Body:	Low-Medium

Food Pairing:

Winner: I only tested breakfasts with skimmed milk.

- 1st for Hard-boiled Eggs, plain Omelette, Scrambled Eggs, Beans on Toast, Mashed Avocado on Toast.
- A glass of cold milk with pair well with chocolate dishes, cakes and biscuits, and spicy dishes (just like yoghurt calms down fiery flavours, milk will do the same)

Loser: Sharp fruit salads and stews.

Jilly from the Taste Team says:

A refreshing, filling and nutritious drink which is surprisingly food friendly. Rediscover your childhood!

MUSCAT / MOSCATO / MOSCATEL

Characteristics

Muscat is a versatile aromatic grape variety (grown for the table and to make raisins as well as wine). It retains its grape smell and taste even after being made into wine. This grape variety can make dry, sweet, fizzy or fortified wines, it is also found in blends (e.g. Tokaji Aszu, sherry).

Grape:	Comes in different colours white, yellow, pink and black: making a white wine.
Origins:	Ancient variety grown throughout the Mediterranean.
Grown:	France, Germany, Italy, Greece, Spain, Switzerland, Australia, South Africa.
Relations:	There are over 200 grape varieties from Muscat, e.g. Muscat Blanc à Petits Grains (arguably makes the most elegant Muscat wines), Brown Muscat, Muscat of Alexandria, etc. The grapes make wines such as Moscato d'Asti, Muscat de Baumes de Venise, Clairette de Die, Muscat de Rivesaltes, sherry, Tokaji Aszu, and Liqueur Muscat.
Acidity:	Low (so drink up quickly unless it's fortified)
Body:	Light-Medium (unless it's fortified)
ABV:	5-19%

Food Pairing

Winner: A Moscato d'Asti DOCG was overall

- 1st in our Puds & Cakes tasting;
- 1st with Scones, Cream & Jam, Banana Cake, Trifle, Bread & Butter Pud, Bakewell Tart;
- =1st with Ginger Cake;
- 3rd with Fried Chicken.

An Orange Muscat from Australia came

- 1st with an Italian Custard Cake.

The barrel-aged, fortified, Liqueur Muscat from Australia came

- 1st for Chocolate Pots;
- =1st with Chocolate Cake.

A Moscatel de Chipiona Sherry came

- 1st with Jam Roly Poly, Fruit Cake, Christmas Pud;
- =1st with Chocolate Cake.

You could also try:

- Muscat de Baumes de Venise with blue cheese with some nuts and dried fruit, and strawberries;
- Dessert Muscat with a chicken liver pâté;
- Muscat de Rivesalte with fruit desserts or sheep cheese;
- Tokaji Aszu is good with blue cheeses, crème caramel, fruity duck, and pumpkin pie.

Loser: Don't mix the lightweight muscats with heavyweight dishes and vice versa.

Maria from the Taste Team says:

Moscato d'Asti is the perfect dessert wine. Not only does it go with sweet dishes, but it is also a light refreshing pick-me-up after a meal.

ORVIETO APPELLATION

Characteristics

Orvieto has a dry fresh white wine, fruity on the nose with a refreshing lemon finish. Pick the DOC level wine.

There is a red wine produced in the area as well as small quantities of off-dry and sweet wines. In fact, in the Middle Ages, Orvieto was renowned for its sweet wines. You're unlikely to come across these in UK supermarkets.

Grape:	A blend of green grapes from Grechetto and Trebbiano plus a few others to make a white wine.
Origins	Italy, around the town of Orvieto in Umbria, extending into Lazio.
Grown:	Italy
Acidity:	Medium-High
Body:	Light - Medium
ABV:	12-13%

Food Pairing

Winner: Orvieto came first with our plain Green Salad and second with our Prawn Cocktail.

Loser: Heavyweight meals will overpower this lightweight wine.

Francis from the Taste Team says:

An easy drinker and great for parties.

PERRY

Characteristics

Pear on the nose and fruity, sweetness on the palate. We tasted an "industrial" perry from a supermarket, which is light bodied and medium sweet. This is quite different from the elegant, craft perries and purists would probably disapprove.

As a drink on its own, the Taste Team found it overly sweet but as a food-friendly accompaniment, it was a revelation and the hit of the tastings.

Fruit:	Perry pears and/or dessert pears.
Origins:	Pear trees were introduced into the UK by the Romans and documentary evidence of perry making comes after the Norman Conquest.
Acidity:	Low-Medium
Tannins:	Low-Medium
Body:	Light
ABV:	4.5%

Food Pairing

Winner: Perry came 1st or =1st for:
- Soups:
  - ◇ Butternut Squash
  - ◇ Leek & potato
  - ◇ Curried Parsnip
  - ◇ Pea & Ham
  - ◇ Minestrone
  - ◇ Mulligatawny
  - ◇ Mushroom

- Sandwiches
  - ◇ Coronation Chicken
  - ◇ Ham & Mustard
  - ◇ Prawn Mayo
  - ◇ Salmon & Cream Cheese Bagel
  - ◇ Cheese & Branston
  - ◇ Chicken & Bacon
- Chicken Vindaloo and Chicken Korma
- Sweet & Sour Pork and 2nd overall for Chinese food
- Salads: Rocket with Spicy Poached Salmon
- Overall winner for Thai food
- 3rd for Cous Cous Salad, Rocket with Poached Salmon,

Loser: cucumber; onion bhajis.

Arti from the Taste Team says:

A perry pear tree can live to over 250 years old. Vintage!

PICPOUL OR PIQUEPOUL

Characteristics

Crisp, lemony, mineral, nutty, dry: a refreshing, crisp white wine. Picpoul de Pinet is one of the few French grape varieties that is also the name of an AOC producing white wines. Elsewhere Picpoul is used as a blend. There is also Picpoul Noir and Picpoul Gris: both of which are used in blends.

Grape	Green grapes making white wine.
Origins	Unknown
Grown	France (Languedoc and Rhône Valley) and Spain
Relations	Unknown
Acidity	Moderate-High
Body	Medium
ABV	Usually 12-13%

Food Pairing

Winner: In the taste tests, Picpoul de Pinet came:
- 1st for Chicken & Bacon Pasta Salad, Cous Cous Salad, Prawn Cocktail, Rocket with Poached Salmon;
- 2nd for BBQ Chicken and Fish Cakes;
- 3rd with Rocket with Spicy Poached Salmon, Salade Niçoise;
- The freshness cuts through the fattiness of a platter of charcuterie, it's good with shellfish and the cheese course too.

Loser: Heavyweight meals such as stews and casseroles.

Nick from the Taste Team says:

A wine that is great value for money. Always useful to have one to hand. Drink young.

PINOT GRIGIO / PINOT GRIS

Characteristics

In Italy, Pinot Grigio grapes are often picked early to maintain acidity resulting in a pretty neutral aroma profile but with a bitter almond undertone. The flavour profile will be lime and green apples with a light body

In Alsace, France, Pinot Gris as it is known there can produce crisp and dry wines or rich and sweet ones so it is wonderfully versatile. If yields are kept in check the wines give off stone fruits, cream and spicy aromas and is quite full-bodied in the Alsace region. These are complex wines with low acidity and quite high alcohol levels. Pinot Gris is considered to be one of the region's noble varieties (along with Riesling and Gewurtztraminer).

This grape variety can produce still dry wines; sparkling dry wines (Crémant d'Alsace) or sweet still wines.

Grape:	Colourful grape (grey, orange, pink, blue – sometimes all on the same bunch) producing white wine
Origins:	Burgundy, France
Grown:	Italy (Veneto), France (Alsace), Austria, Germany, Luxembourg, Hungary, USA, Australia, Argentina, Moldova, New Zealand.
Relations:	Mutation from Pinot Noir
Acidity:	Med-high
Body:	Light-med
ABV:	Typically 12.5-13.5%

Food Pairing

Winner: Pinot Gris: sushi, dim sum, Chinese foods. Pinot Grigio (served at about 7°C): Gruyère cheese, fresh veggies, fish, seafood, chicken and turkey. Wines from the USA and Australia will complement creamy, richer dishes as the alcohol content will be higher.

Loser: Red meats, stews, hearty foodstuffs

Arti from the Taste Team says:
If the label says Pinot Grigio, then expect a dry, neutral wine. If it says Pinot Gris, expect more aroma and flavour.

PINOT NOIR

Characteristics

Strawberry, cherry and other red fruits. Always pale and delicate – its colour is light red. Aged in barrel, the mature specimen is much more complex and elegant with layers of herbaceous undergrowth, farmyard and gaminess.

Pinot Noir is a tricky customer to grow: when it's good, it's off the scale; when it's bad, it is bad, bad, bad. The plant prefers a cool climate – yet it often fails to ripen. In a warm climate, it'll ripen too soon. Wherever it's grown, it still manages to express its terroir – that combination of soil, climate, grower and wine maker.

On the vine, the bunch is a mass of grapes (pinot supposedly coming from the word for pine cone) – a haven for any number of diseases let alone rot, and the grapes are thin skinned too. All this requires careful handling. Pinot Noir is like the Holy Grail to viticulturists and wine makers: if you can get it right, it's Heaven on Earth.

Pinot Noir is also a crucial ingredient in Blanc de Noirs Champagnes.

Grape:	Black grapes making red wine and white sparkling wines (usually part of a blend)
Origins:	Burgundy, France
Grown:	France, USA, NZ, Chile, Argentina, Australia, Germany, Italy, South Africa, Austria
Relations:	Parent of Chardonnay, Gamay, Melon de Bourgogne, mutations led to Pinot Gris, Pinot Blanc and Pinot Meunier
Acidity:	Medium-High
Body:	Light-Medium

Tannins:	Low to high (if whole bunch maceration is carried out, the stalks add significant tannins)
Oak:	Frequent
ABV:	11-14%

Food Pairing

Winner: Young, unoaked, fresh wines will go with lighter dishes: patés and terrines, quiches, sandwiches. 2nd with BBQ Burgers, BBQ Pork Chops, Veggie Kebabs. 3rd for BBQ Salmon, Cheeseburger, Hot-dog and, when chilled, Seafood Kebabs.

An older Burgundy came 1st with Roast Chicken, Roast Turkey, Roast Pork and Roast Pheasant. Try also mushroom dishes and rabbit.

An American Pinot Noir was voted 1st to go with Thai Green Curry and 3rd with Ginger Beef and Chicken Vindaloo, so it can take a little spice (when unoaked).

Loser: salty foods; heavily spiced dishes; too many flavours and spices will overwhelm Pinot Noir.

Jilly from the Taste Team says:

My absolute favourite grape variety. If you've got a spare slice of home-made chicken pie and a nice glass of Pinot Noir, just call me, I'll be there.

PORTER

Characteristics

Porter has a complex taste including fruit (especially dried fruit such as raisin or sultana), liquorice, chocolate, coffee, molasses and hop bitterness. A real depth of flavour and rich mouthfeel.

Grain:	Barley. Using a pale malt base with, typically, a mix of Crystal, Brown, Chocolate, and Black malts to make the dark brown to black colour and complex flavours, yet easy on the hops.
Origins:	First documented in London in the 1720s, Porter is believed to be named after the London porters and river porters who needed nutritional refreshment, although the Porter of those times was a lot stronger than ones today. Its recipe has evolved over the centuries but, using London's rich-in-carbonate water, English hops and yeast, London Porter consistently wins awards throughout the world.
IBU:	20-60
Body:	Medium to Full
ABV:	4-7%

Food Pairing

Winner:
- =1st for Mince Pies;
- 2nd for Christmas Pud
- Did quite well with a Pork Sausage & Mustard;
  - *3rd for Roast Beef;*
  - *Try also, oxtail casserole, steak 'n' ale pie, stilton, roast wild boar.*

Loser: It didn't work well with our sandwiches, particularly those will a creamy/mayonnaise dressing.

Jilly from the Taste Team says:

I love a London Porter and what better excuse to eat just one more Mince Pie.

2016©

RIESLING

Characteristics

One of the aromatic grape varieties. When young, citrus, apples and a whiff of petrol dominate. More exotic fruits (mango, guava, peach) appear in Rieslings from warmer climates.

The vine itself is very woody so thrives in cooler climates, where the grape maintains its acidity until the end of the growing season. It is heavily influenced by the place it is grown, so expresses its terroir well. The wines can age phenomenally well.

Grape:	White grape making aromatic white wines, from dry to sweet.
Origins:	Rhine region of Germany
Grown:	Germany, France, Austria, Australia, USA, Canada
Relations:	Resulting from a cross between Gouais Blanc and a wild grape crossed with one of the Traminers.
Acidity:	High
Body:	Light - Medium
ABV:	10-13%

Food Pairing

New World Riesling winners:

- 1st with BBQ Salmon;
- 3rd for BBQ Chops and BBQ Halloumi.

Off-dry Rieslings winners:

- 1st for Aromatic Crispy Duck, Chicken & Cashew Nuts and Egg Fried Rice;
- Overall first for Chinese takeaway;
- =1st with Mushroom Soup
- 1st for Chip Butty with Ketchup
- 2nd for Tomato & Mozzarella Salad, Cheese & Branston Sandwich, Chicken & Bacon Sarnie, Chip Butty, Prawn Mayo Sandwich, Smoked Salmon & Cream Cheese Sandwich, Mushroom Soup; Bangers & Mash, Cheeseburger, Singapore Noodles, Sweet & Sour Pork and Fish & Chips;
- 3rd with Fish Finger Sandwich, Salmon Fillet, Crispy Beef and Sushi.

The sweeter Rieslings would marry well with desserts and cakes, chicken parfait, or salty cheeses.

Loser: Dry and very sweet Rieslings with Asian food (off-dry is best). Heavyweight, red meat dishes.

Nick from the Taste Team says:

There are so many different styles of Riesling to choose from. Dry/Kabinett/Trocken, to Off Dry/Halbtrocken, to Sweet/ Beerenauslese and Eiswein/Ice Wine. Some wines labelled Spätlese and Auslese can be dry, off-dry or sweet depending on the desire of the winemaker. Make a note of the Rieslings you like.

RIOJA APPELLATION

Characteristics

There are four types of Rioja for both red and white wine:

- Rioja: the entry level: fresh and fruity with just a little ageing in oak barrels or none. Probably one or two years old.
- Crianza: this wine spends 1 year in oak barrels and 1 year ageing in the bottle. White wines must spend 6 months in the barrel.
- Reserva: specially selected grapes, aged for 3 years, 1 year in oak barrels (whites: 2 years ageing, 6 months in oak).
- Gran Reserva: only made in exceptional years, these wines must be aged for at least 5 years before release, 2 of which must be in oak barrels. The whites must be aged for 4 years, 1 of which in oak. These wines have great ageing potential.

Grape:	A blend of principally Tempranillo (at least 60%), Garnacha (Grenache) and other authorised grape varieties to make red wine. Or a blend of Viura (Macabeo), Garnacha Blanca and Vedejo to make white wine; Garnacha for rosé.
Origins:	Named after La Rioja region in Northern Spain and now a DOCa appellation (rules and regulations should lead to higher quality wines).
Acidity:	Medium-High
Body:	Medium-Full
Tannins:	Medium
Oak:	No for the entry level Riojas, yes to the other reds.
ABV:	12-14%

This red wine is recognised for its structure, fruit and tannins and ageing potential for the top wines. The white wine is fruity, fresh, with good structure; when oaked the wines develop a nuttiness and complexity which makes them excellent food wines. You might also find rosé wines from Rioja, usually made from Garnacha. These are refreshing wines for an apéritif and designed to be drunk young.

Food Pairing

With so many styles in Rioja wine, a definitive answer is tricky but try these:

- Whites: unoaked: apéritif, light lunches
- Whites: oaked: swordfish, tuna, chicken, pork, turkey, veal
- Rosé: a picnic is summer; light lunches
- Reds: Meats, BBQs, tapas, strong cheeses

Winner: We tested:
- An unoaked, fresh, White Rioja which came
  - ◇ 1st overall in our Italian tasting;
  - ◇ 1st for Chicken Milanese;
- A red Rioja came
  - ◇ 2nd with our BBQ Sausages.
- A Rioja Reserva came
  - ◇ 1st for Shepherd's Pie;
  - ◇ 2nd with Cottage Pie, Cumberland Pie and Roast Lamb;
  - ◇ 3rd with Roast Chicken Pie.

Loser: Avoid delicate foodstuffs with the reds; the whites and rosés won't shine with robust dishes.

Maria from the Taste Team says:

If the Rioja you've chosen doesn't marry well with what you're eating, put a stopper in, keep the bottle cool and in the dark, and match your next meal to the wine.

ROSÉ, ROSADO OR ROSATO WINES

Characteristics

Rosés can be virtually just cold and wet to fruity wines with some body. Try the rosés from Bandol, France, Navarra, Spain and the Portuguese rosés with food. The colour comes either from:

- A short contact with the skins during crushing (1-3 days).
- If juice is removed at an early stage of black-grape pressing, the resulting red wine has more tannins and a bigger colour. The by-product (the pink juice) is fermented separately to make a rosé. This is the saignée or bleeding off method, e.g. rosé Champagne.
- It might also come from blending red and white wine but this practice is frowned upon and even illegal in some countries.

Grape:	Any black-skinned grape can be used; the resulting colour will vary from pale salmon to red
Grown:	France, Spain, Italy, Portugal, USA, in fact every wine producing country
Styles:	Still, semi-sparking or sparkling; dry to sweet
ABV:	12.5% to 15%

Food Pairing

- 1st for Ham Omelette, Salade Niçoise and Salmon Fillet
- 2nd for BBQ Chicken, Caesar Salad, Hot Dog, Jacket Potato with Coleslaw, Rogan Josh, Seafood Kebabs
- 3rd for Aromatic Crispy Duck, Balti, BBQ, Chicken Tikka Masala, Chicken Vindaloo, Lamp Chops, Singapore Noodles, Sweet & Sour Pork, Tomato & Mozzarella Salad.

Loser: Meaty stews and casseroles.

Maria from the Taste Team says:

Keep the delicate, cold and wet rosés for your apéritif. Use a bolder wine with food.

SANGIOVESE

Characteristics

On its own, you'll find Sangiovese has medium colour, aromas of fresh cherries, plum, herbs, notes of spice, smoke, nuttiness and savoury. Older versions will tend towards figs, pot pourri, and dried cherries too.

You'll more often than not find Sangiovese as part of a blend (think Chianti). Blending adds body and texture to the wine, which complements the lighter-bodied Sangiovese.

The quality of wine making has improved markedly in recent decades and now with lower yields (so more concentrated grapes) and more attention to wine making, Sangiovese is coming into its own.

If it's a special occasion and your wallet is fat Brunello di Montalcino DOCG.

Grape:	Black-skinned grape making red wine
Origins:	Italy. The name derives from "Sangue di Giove" (blood of Jove) a reference to Jupiter, which, many suggest, means this grape was around in Roman times.
Grown:	Italy, Italy, Italy by far. Small plantings, some experimental, in France (Corsica), Argentina, USA, Australia, Chile.
Relations:	Probably a cross of Ciliegiolo from Tuscany and Calabrese Montenuovo from Southern Italy.
Acidity:	High
Body:	Light-Medium
Tannins:	High
Oak:	Frequently
ABV:	12.5% to 15%

Food Pairing

Winner:
- 1st Pasta Carbonara;
- 2nd Pizza;
- Our Chianti Classico (predominantly Sangiovese) came 1st for Spag Bol and 1st for Pasta & Pesto.
- Renown for marrying well with tomato-based dishes; try also with meatloaf, roasted meats, rich chicken or mushroom dishes and steak.

Loser: Fried foods (battered or crumbed), seafood (except if it's with a tomato-based sauce).

Arti from the Taste Team says:

*If you're lucky enough to come across a **Vino Nobile di Montepulicano DOCG**, this wine is dominated by Sangiovese and named after the village not the Montepulciano grape variety from the Abruzzo region in Italy.*

SAUVIGNON BLANC

Characteristics

Not only is the vine grown throughout the world, surely you can get a glass of Sauvignon Blanc in the UK. It's everywhere and I don't mean that as a complement. A tasting at NZ House revealed 132 different wines made from Sauvignon Blanc: the majority of these were damn fine.

Green pepper, nettles, grass (herbaceous) is what you'll get when the dry wine comes from a cool climate. This grape variety can grow in warmer climates but there needs to be a cooling influence (altitude, wind, water) otherwise the acidity and aromas will disappear and the wine will be disappointing. When it's successful though you can expect gooseberry, and riper, more tropical fruits.

When Sauvignon Blanc is blended with, for example, sémillon in Bordeaux (Sauternes and Barsac), it makes a wonderful dessert wine, which ages so well. Expect a thick, viscous wine, with orange, marmalade and citrus but this sweetness is well balanced by the acidity.

This combination of sémillon and Sauvignon Blanc can also be aged in oak in Pessac-Léognan and Graves, both in the Bordeaux area of France. This dry wine will have a fuller mouthfeel with toasty, nutty notes.

One of our favourite wines for desserts (see that section) was Monbazillac: a blend of Sémillon, Sauvignon Blanc, and Muscadelle. This sweet wine comes from vineyards around the village of Monbazillac, near Bergerac in SW France.

Grape:	Green grapes making white wine
Origins:	Not proven but either the Loire or Bordeaux, France
Grown:	France, Chile, South Africa, USA, Italy, Australia, Spain, Brazil, Slovenia, Czech Rep, Moldova, Serbia, Austria, Slovenia and notably New Zealand: a truly international grape variety.
Relations:	Offspring of Sauvignon Blanc and unknown, and parent to Cabernet Sauvignon, probably related to Chenin Blanc, Traminer, Grüner Veltliner, Verdesse, Verdejo blanco and Verdelho da Madeira.
Acidity:	High
Body:	Mainly light-medium (except when sweet or oaked)
ABV:	Usually 12-13%

Food Pairing

Winner: Sauvignon Blanc is a versatile food wine. Find your favourite style. Here are our findings:

- Goats cheese and a glass of Sancerre is a classic combination;
- Sancerre was the top choice with an omelette;
- Fish and the lighter style of wine from the Eastern Loire, which are very good value for money, go well too;
- A Sancerre came 3rd with Green Thai Curry and Pad Thai;
- Sauvignon Blanc came 1st with Mashed Avocado on Toast; Peanut Butter on Toast, Waffle;
- 2nd with Chicken & Bacon Pasta Salad, Cous Cous Salad, Ham Hock, Egg & Potato Salad and Salmon en Croûte;
- 3rd with Chicken Caesar Salad and Sushi.
- A fruity, crisp Sauvignon Blanc from California was overall top choice in our Soups & Sarnies Part 3. It also came first for pairing with BLT, Beef & Horseradish, Marmite & Watercress sandwiches, then French Onion Soup;
- 2nd with Oxtail Soup.

Loser: avoid anything spicy, bitter, sweet, heavyweight meat dishes.

Arti from the Taste Team says:

Wherever it's grown, a basic dry Sauvignon Blanc is a wine designed to be drunk young – so enjoy!

© Theresa Harrow, Honest Grapes

SWEET WINES

Characteristics

Sweet Wines, dessert wines, stickies – they tend to be grouped together at the supermarket, often on the top shelf. I find myself standing there like a child in an old-fashioned sweetshop.

Here's a brief description of the different styles you might come across. They all have their place so enjoy experimenting. Which one will you choose?

Fortified Wines

Fermentation is stopped by the addition of a spirit (grape spirit, brandy, etc.) leaving some of the sugars un-fermented. If all the sugars are fermented the wine will be dry (e.g. some sherries). The spirit helps preserve the wine. These wines, including Port, Sherry, and Madeira, are typically around 20% ABV. See individual entry for Tawny Port. These wines need full-bodied foods otherwise they'll overpower your dishes.

Ice Wine/Eiswein

A spell of very cold weather (-7/8°C) after the grapes have ripened is required. It's only the water in the grapes that freezes, so when pressed, the juices are highly concentrated. The harvest is dependent upon weather conditions, the birds not eating the berries, and the berries not dropping. The harvest is carried out by hand with the pickers wearing thick gloves, and the cellar workers wear many layers as their workplace has to be unheated. The result is an unctuous, smooth, sweet wine that still retains some acidity.

I happened to have a Georgian ice wine in my "cellar" which I used in a couple of the Tea Time & Puds tastings. When I checked the price of it, unfortunately it's not available in this country. In fact, I couldn't find an ice wine in a supermarket so you might need to go to an independent vintner. For a special occasion, you can't do better.

Late Harvest Wines

These wines come from ripe grapes, which have been left on the vine so that the berries dry and the sugars become concentrated.

On the bottle labels, you'll find Spâtlese and Auslese for German wines; Vendange Tardive for French or Late Harvest elsewhere.

Noble Rot

If the conditions are right, ripe grapes will suffer from Noble Rot – the Botrytis cinerea fungus. These grapes are so prized that they are often picked berry by berry, indeed mechanical harvesting is banned in some areas. The wine produced is fine, concentrated and sweet. This type of wine is usually a blend of different grape varieties.

If you ever get the chance to taste a Hungarian Tokaji Aszu, you won't regret it. Bordeaux's famous Sauternes is absolutely delicious and has a price-tag to match; the more affordable Monbazillac from SW France has a better price/quality ratio for normal mortals' palates. Beerenauslese and Trockenbeerenauslese Rieslings also suffer from Noble Rot, as do Sélection de Grains Nobles in Alsace for Gewürztraminer, Pinot Gris, Riesling or Muscat.

Off-Dry Wines

Fermentation has been stopped early so that some residual sugar remains.

Vins Doux Naturels

French wines made from Muscat or Grenache. Up to 10% grape spirit is added during fermentation, which stops it. So these wines are lightly fortified. Examples are Muscat de Beaumes de Venise and Banyuls (see individual entry).

Grape:	Muscat, Riesling, Gewürztraminer, Grenache, Blends (sémillon, Muscadelle, Sauvignon Blanc)
Origins:	A sweet wine was produced from raisins in ancient Carthage.
Grown:	Canada (Icewine); Germany (Eiswein and Rieslings); France, and most other wine producing countries.
Acidity:	Medium
Body:	Light to full
ABV:	7-16%

Food Pairing

Winner: these wines don't only go with sweet treats (see the Tea Time & Puds Chapter where they really shine). Try also with:
- Chicken liver parfait;
- Chicken livers,
- Hard cheeses
- Off-dry wines were good with Asian food, particularly if you want the same wine for the whole meal.

Loser: If the food is sweeter than the wine, any acidity of the wine will be emphasised.

Maria from the Taste Team says:

Taking a bottle of wine as a gift to your host is standard practice. But your host might have carefully selected the wines to drink. Often overlooked is a dessert wine. Take a chilled bottle and you'll be highly thought of!

SYRAH / SHIRAZ

Characteristics

This grape variety has two common names. Syrah, the original name, is how it's known in France. In Australia, it's called Shiraz. Wines from this grape variety will show different character aspects depending where it's grown.

In cooler climates (e.g. France), expect blackberry, mint, trademark black pepper, high acidity, and big tannins.

In hotter regions (e.g. Australia), you'll find jammy fruit and lots of it, softer tannins and chocolate notes, liquorice, anise and earthy leather, and higher alcohol. Both styles have the potential to age well.

Wines from countries might be labelled Syrah if they're in the French style, and Shiraz in the Australian.

You'll find Syrah as a single varietal wine as well as in a blend, notably GSM (Grenache, Syrah/Shiraz, Mourvèdre) from the Southern Rhône (e.g. Côtes du Rhône blend) and Australia, or it can be blended with Cabernet Sauvignon.

Australian wine makers experiment with Shiraz and you might come across a sparkling wine, rosé and fortified wines.

Grape:	Black-skinned grape making red wine
Origins:	Northern Rhône, France
Grown:	France, Italy, Spain, Portugal, Australia, New Zealand, Chile, Argentina, USA, and South Africa
Relations:	Offspring of Dureza and Mondeuse Blanche

Acidity:	Medium to High
Body:	Full
Tannins:	High
Oak:	Frequently
ABV:	13.5%-15%

Food Pairing

Winner: Our Côte du Rhône blend came:

- 1st for Sausages with Onion Gravy;
- As a single varietal, it came first with BBQ Lamb Chops, Cottage Pie, Cumberland Pie and BBQ Steak;
- 2nd with Shepherd's Pie;
- 3rd for Steak & Mushroom Pie.
- Syrah/Shiraz has an affinity with Lamb, BBQs, slow roasted Pork, stews, game and hearty winter fare.

Loser: This wine will overpower lighter dishes such as fish and salads.

Sean from the Taste Team says:

If you see Syrah on the label, the wine has probably been made in an Old World style; if it's Shiraz, then it'll be New World style and higher in alcohol.

TAWNY PORT

Characteristics

Aromas of dried fruit, nuts, marmalade, sweet spices. Intense and persistent on the palate, fruit and nuts, big mouth feel. Different varieties of grapes are fermented: all of the grapes used have to be on the authorised list but the wine maker isn't obliged to use every grape variety listed.

The fermentation is stopped by the addition of alcohol (thus leaving residual sugar). This wine is then aged in wooden barrels (remember the pipes of port Godfathers would buy their Godchildren back in the day?). Over time, oxidation takes place and the wine becomes more and more tawny in colour.

The official ages for port are no age indication (I avoid these bulk wines), 10, 20, 30, and Over 40 years' ageing. If, for example, 20 years is stated on the label, then this is simply an indication of the age as the wine will be blended from barrels from different years. The resulting Tawny Port will reflect the port house's style.

Grape:	A blend of over 70 authorised black grapes, e.g. Tinta Barroca, Touriga Franca, Tinta da Barca and Rufete, fortified and aged in oak to make a sweet or medium dry, fortified wine.
Origins:	Portugal. In the 18th Century, French ports were blockaded by the Royal Navy and French wines were heavily taxed. To satisfy the thirst of the nation, Portuguese wines were purchased instead, and, in order to preserve them on their journey to Blighty, a local brandy was added.
Acidity:	Medium - High
Tannins:	Medium - High
Oak:	Yes
Body:	Full
ABV:	19-21%

We didn't test other styles of port but you'll find ruby, reserve/reserva, LBV (late bottled vintage), white, colheita, vintage port on the supermarket shelf, particularly at Christmas time.

Food Pairing

Winner: Tawny Port came:

- 1st with Salted Caramel ice Cream;
- 2nd with Lobster Bisque, Beef & Horseradish Sandwich, Chocolate Cake, Coconut Ice Cream;
- 3rd with Marmite & Watercress sarnie.
- We also feel this wine would pair well with nutty tart, plum pudding, lamb or chicken liver (don't forget to de-glaze the pan with a dash of Tawny) and hard cheeses.

Loser: Light fish dishes would be lost with this complex wine.

Francis from the Taste Team says:

Try lightly chilling a Tawny Port and drink as an apéritif, comme les Français!

TEMPRANILLO / TINTO RORIZ

Characteristics

Rarely found as a single varietal wine, Tempranillo brings alcohol, strawberries, cherries, spice and perhaps leather and tobacco to blends. It is the key component in Rioja wines (see separate entry), wines from the Ribera del Duero in Spain, as well as trendy, great value for money Portuguese wines. It can also be one of the grape varieties, which makes Port.

In Northern Portugal, particularly in the Douro and the Dão, Tempranillo is known as Tinto Roriz. In Southern Portugal, it is known as Aragonez or Arinto Tinto.

Its blending partners are often Grenache (Garnacha), Carignan (Mazuela), Touriga Naçional, Touriga Franca

Grape:	Black-skinned grape making red wine.
Origins:	Spain
Grown:	Spain, Portugal, USA, Argentina, South Africa
Acidity:	Low-Moderate
Body:	Medium
ABV:	13%-14.5%

Food Pairing

Winner: Robust dishes; roasted meats, BBQs, tapas, Beef Wellington, stews, strong cheeses

Loser: lightweight lunches and picnics

Penny from the Taste Team says:

Hearty and robust, a perfect match for a winter casserole before settling down with the Sunday papers for 40 winks!

TORRONTÉS

Characteristics

Aromatic grape variety, with heady floral scents of jasmine, then citrus, hint of honey, and peppery spice. The smell is such that you think this wine will be sweet but, no, this is a dry white wine with a refreshing acidity.

Grape:	White
Origins:	Native to Argentina – their signature white grape variety
Grown:	Argentina
Relations:	Chance cross between Criolla Chica (Mission) and Muscat of Alexandria. Not related to the Spanish Torrontés
Acidity:	High
Body:	Light-medium
ABV:	12-14%

Food Pairing

Winner: This wine had several successes in our tastings:

- 1st with Mozzarella, Tomato & Basil salad and 1st with Singapore Noodles.
- 2nd for Rocket with Spicy Poached Salmon and Waldorf Salad.
- 3rd for Prawn Cocktail.
- Try also with traditional hot meat empanadas.

Loser: Meaty stews would overpower this wine.

Nick from the Taste Team says:

Great value for money wine, which is food friendly and a crowd pleaser.

VERMENTINO

Characteristics

Fruit and floral aromas with citrus, then a persistent follow through in the mouth. The most famous Vermentino is the Vermentino di Gallura DOCG from northern Sardinia. You might come across a sweet or a sparkling style but you'd have to search for them.

Grape:	Pale grape making white wine.
Origins:	Unknown. Rumours abound – why not make one up?
Grown:	Italy, particularly Sardinia, France, USA, Australia
Relations:	Unknown
Acidity:	Medium-High
Body:	Medium
ABV:	12-13%

Food Pairing

Winner: This wine came:

- =1st with our Pasta Carbonara;
- 1st for the Mushroom Ravioli;
- Other creamy pasta dishes would work as would chicken.
- It came 2nd with Prawns.

Loser: Hearty fare would be too much for this wine.

Arti from the Taste Team says:

The acidity of the wine cuts through the fats in the dish leaving a delicious, complementary mouthfeel.

WHEAT BEER

Characteristics

Wheat beers contain 30-70% wheat malt, the rest being barley malt or sometimes oats. It's a top-fermented beer and brewed all over the world these days so styles are varied, but the two well-known ones are Weissbier and Witbier.

The wheat, whilst not contributing much to the flavour, gives a smooth mouthfeel to the beer. Make sure you pour your beer into a glass rather than necking a bottle; the sediment should be poured too – this type of beer is usually cloudy. The head will allow you to appreciate all the aromas in the drink: often coriander with citrus after notes.

Effervescence is high so particularly refreshing. Synonymous with summertime. With its low hop bitterness, it's easy to pair with food.

Origins	Germany (but the Netherlands, Belgium claim it too).
Body	Light
IBU	Around 15
ABV	4%-6%

Food Pairing

Winner:

- 1st with Korma, Rogan Josh, Chicken Jalfrezi and Madras;
- 2nd with Balti, and Chicken Tikka Masala;
- 3rd with a plain Green Salad, Chicken & Bacon Pasta Salad, Cheese & Branston Sandwich, Chicken & Bacon Sandwich, Pea & Ham soup, BBQ Chicken, Fish Cakes and Prawns.

Loser: Hearty fare, like Snake & Pygmy, won't show the beer at its best.

Penny from the Taste Team says:

Wheat Beer is very versatile: from a light lunch to an Indian Take Away. I always have some in my stash.

ZINFANDEL / PRIMITIVO

Characteristics

You'll find characteristics of bramble fruits, blueberry, cherry; black pepper and liquorice.

It was thanks to DNA profiling in the 1990s that the origins of Zinfandel were found. It's not native to California, USA, where this grape variety is the second-most planted black grape vine. It originally came from Croatia where the pronounceable name is Tribidrag (if you want the unpronounceable name, it's Crljenak Kastelanski). Profiling also discovered that these two varieties are the same as Primitivo, grown in Puglia, Italy.

Grape:	Black grape making red wine.
Origins:	Croatia
Grown:	USA principally California, Italy (in Puglia), Croatia and Montegnegro
Relations:	Same DNA as Tribidrag from Montenegro and Primitivo from Italy
Styles:	Dry light reds, hearty reds, rosé (called White Zinfandel, this wine although available in supermarkets wasn't tasted in our tests), late harvest dessert wines, fortified wines
Acidity:	Medium-High
Body:	Light-Full
Tannins:	Medium-High
Oak:	The big, heavyweight reds are normally oaked.
ABV:	Usually 14-17%

Food Pairing

Winner: A Californian Zinfandel came

- 1st for BBQ Ribs;
- 2nd for BBQ Lamb Chops and Roast Duck;
- 3rd for BBQ Sausages and BBQ Steak.
- Try also with Roast Goose, and game stews.

Loser: Delicate dishes will be swamped by this red wine.

Arti from the Taste Team says:

If you're having a BBQ, pick this for your red wine. A crowd pleaser and a screw cap!

FURTHER INFORMATION

There is a lot of information out there on the web: some more reliable than others. I've found these sites to be particularly interesting or useful:

Australian Wine
Everything you need to know about wines from Australia
http://www.wineaustralia.net.au/en/wine-regions.aspx

Austrian Wine
Everything you need to know about wines from Austria
http://www.austrianwine.com

CAMRA
The Campaign for Real Ale.
http://www.camra.org.uk

Canadian Vintners
Everything you need to know about wines from Canada
http://www.canadianvintners.com

Corks Out
Independent wine and spirit specialists, with tasting machines, wines available by the glass and light bites. Based in the North of England – lucky you if you live nearby.
http://www.corksout.com

Drink Aware
All the facts and figures about the dangers of drinking acohol.
https://www.drinkaware.co.uk

Foodpairing
The science behind pairings
https://www.foodpairing.com/en/home

Foods & Wines from Spain
All you need to know about foods and wines from Spain
http://www.foodswinesfromspain.com

Honest Grapes
Independent on-line wine merchant, seller of Taste Lab Kits to help you discover your taste profile, likes and dislikes.
www.honestgrapes.co.uk

Jancis Robinson
Wine critic, journalist, wine writer and Master of Wine. What this highly-respected lady doesn't know about wine isn't worth knowing.
http://www.jancisrobinson.com

NZ Wine
Everything you need to know about wines from New Zealand
http://www.nzwine.com

Quaffing & Scoffing
Updates on food and drink matching. Join the discussion
http://www.quaffingandscoffing.co.uk
Facebook: Quaffing & Scoffing
Twitter: @Quaff_n_Scoff.

The Wine Society
The world's oldest wine club. It's a co-operative and you need to buy one share to join. Consulting the website is free though and it's full of useful information. I find the wines are excellent and good value for money. The Wine Society organises tastings around the country.
http://www.thewinesociety.com

UK Sommelier Association
My alma mater
http://www.uksommelierassociation.com

Vinotech Pty Ltd (winesave)
Producer of canisters of argon gas to keep your half-empty bottles in pristine condition. Highly recommended.
http://www.winesave.com

Wine Folly
If you're a visual person, check out this American site with lots of graphics.
http://winefolly.com

Wines of Argentina
Everything you need to know about Argentinian wines
http://www.winesofargentina.com

Wines of Chile
Everything you need to know about Chilean wines
http://www.winesofchile.org

Wines of Germany
Everything you need to know about German wines
http://www.winesofgermany.co.uk

Wines of Portugal
Everything you need to know about Portuguese wines
http://www.winesofportugal.info

Wines of South Africa
Everything you need to know about South African wines
http://www.winesofsa.co.uk

Wines of the USA
No one overall site., Go by region:
http://www.discovercalifornawines.co.uk
http://www.oregonwine.org
http://washingtonwine.org

Wineware
Glasses, spittoons, wine coolers, and a wealth of information, Wineware is friendly, efficient and my suppliers of choice.
https://www.wineware.co.uk

Wine Tours
Formerly Arblaster & Clarke Wine Tours (known as Half Plastered & Parked), if you fancy exploring a wine country or region, you couldn't do better than go with Wine Tours. They're friendly, efficient and nothing's too much trouble.
http://winetours.co.uk

GLOSSARY

ABV: Alcohol By Volume

A.O.C.: See Appellation d'Origine Controlée

Acid: You'll find acid in all grapes and it is an essential part of wine. Acid helps a wine age by maintaining its freshness, it enlivens the wine and helps prolong its aftertaste. If a wine is too acidic then it is unbalanced. Appropriate food pairing can lessen the apparent acidity. In a hot year, there will be less acidity; in a cool, rainy year, there will be higher acidity.

Aeration: You aerate a wine by either pulling out the cork and letting the wine breathe, decanting the bottle into another vessel or simply swirling the wine in your glass. Your aim is to get the wine to relax and release its aromas. Be careful though with old and delicate wines as these wines might lose all their fruity aromas.

Aftertaste: After you've swallowed (or spat out) the wine, the aftertaste is the flavours that linger in the mouth. The length of the aftertaste is called the finish, length or persistence. A fine wine will have a long aftertaste.

Ageing: Most everyday wines are made to be drunk within a year or two of release as the quality will not improve and will actually deteriorate with age. Finer wines can improve with age. You'll need a wine that has sufficient acidity, alcohol and tannins, cool and stable storage conditions. These wines will develop additional complexity in the bottle.

Aggressive: Aggressive wines are unpleasant due to their high acidity and/or tannins.

Alcohol: Ethyl alcohol is a by-product of the yeasts feeding on the grapes' sugar during fermentation.

Alcohol by volume (ABV): Required by law, ABV is usually expressed as a percentage, e.g. 12.5%.

Alcoholic: You can smell if a wine is alcoholic, and the aftertaste will be hot or heavy. Alcoholic wines are unbalanced, so a negative characteristic.

Ampelography: The study and identification of grape varieties.

Appellation: Referring to an area, which has rules and regulations regarding its viticulture and viniculture.

Appellation d'Origine Contrôlée (AOC) This term has been replaced by the Appelation d'Origine Protegée (AOP). This French system protects areas by name and specifies the rules and regulations regarding its viticulture (e.g. varieties used, ripeness, yields) and how the wine is made

Aroma: Smell, generally pleasant unless specified otherwise.

Astringent: If you get a furry or drying sensation in your mouth, this comes from the tannins. If the tannins are high (e.g. from a young wine), then the wine can be described as astringent. Astringency can be a wine fault or just that the wine is too young to drink or part of a complex wine.

Austere: A wine that is unapproachable and not particularly nice to drink can be austere. It lacks roundness and depth in the mouth. Often applied to wines which are too young to drink but which will mellow and evolve with time.

Balance: The Holy Grail of wine where the wine's sugar, alcohol and polyalcohol are balanced by the wine's acidity, tannins and minerality.

Big: A big wine is a full-bodied wine, with intensity, persistence and concentration, e.g. Malbec.

Blend: a wine made from more than one grape variety.

Body: the weight of a wine: light, medium or full. Match the body of the wine with the weight of the food.

Bouquet: the smell of the wine, particularly a bottle-aged, evolved wine, which smells more than just grape.

Cellaring Wine is perishable and should be looked after carefully if you want to keep it a long time. Cool and dark are the most important factors. Humidity, avoiding large and sudden temperature variations and vibrations also play a part.

Clarification: wine making process to remove of insoluble material (e.g. dead yeast cells) to make the wine clear bright

Complex: An interesting wine, which has layers of different smells and tastes.

Corked: A serious wine fault resulting in a smell of mouldy cellars and damp cardboard. The wine has been contaminated by a chemical called trichloroanisole (TCA), a reaction between chlorine and cork. Do not drink this wine: most retailers will replace it or refund your money. Cork floaters in the wine do not lead to corked wine.

Crémant: a French sparkling wine, which isn't make in Champagne.

Decanting: Pouring the wine from its bottle to another container, usually a decanter. This is done firstly to remove any sediment in the wine, and secondly, and more controversially, to allow the wine to breathe. Some claim decanting makes the wine's smell dissipate, others claim the wine opens up better.

Delicate: Refers to light, usually white, wines

DO: Denominación de Origen is Spain's designation for wines

DOC: Denominazione di Origine Controllata is Italy's designation for wines

DOC: Denominaçao de Origem Controlada is Portugal's designation for wines

DOCG: Denominazaione di Origine Controllata e Garantita is Italy's designation for its top wines

Dulce/Doux/Dolce/Doce: Spanish, French, Italian and Portuguese terms for a sweet wine

Dry: not sweet. The vast majority of wines are dry.

Eiswein: German for ice wine – a dessert wine made from frozen grapes.

Elevé en fûts de chêne: French term for aged in oak barrels

Elegant: A wine that is not in your face but which has complexity, great balance and sophistication.

Extracted: Imagine the tea bag in your cup of tea: if you press and leave the bag to steep, your cuppa will be stronger and more tannic. The same with wine. The colour and flavour from wines comes from the skins, pips and sometimes the stalks. The term over extracted tends to take on negative connotations and you would expect a dense, very tannic or even bitter wine. .

Fermentation: the process of yeast eating the sugars in the grape juice and producing alcohol.

Filtration The removal of suspended solid particles in a wine by passing it through a filter. Expect an unfiltered wine to have sediment.

Fine Wine: top quality wine

Fining: the wine making process of adding a product (and then removing it) to make the wine clear.

Finish: describes the flavours left over after swallowing or spitting. It also refers to how persistent a wine's flavour is in the mouth: short or long.

Flabby: A wine which lacks acidity to balance the other elements.

Flinty: Literally the smell of flint, often a characteristic of young Chablis

Floral: A smell reminiscent of flowers (white flowers, yellow flowers or specific varieties, e.g. honeysuckle, rose)

Fortified Wine: Wine to which spirit has been added. Liquoroso in Italian and vin de Liqueur in French.

Fresh: A wine, usually white, with some acidity which is often light and refreshingly pleasant. A good match with many foods.

Frizzante: Italian wine term for a semi-sparkling wine.

Fruity: A smell reminiscent of fruit (e.g. blackcurrant, apricot, lemon).

Full-bodied: Heavy weight wines full of extract, alcohol and glycerol and, for red wines, tannins.

Geographical Indication: a World Trade Organization description of a wine region producing wines with defined characteristics (e.g. AOP in France, DOC in Italy)

Grand Cru: French term for "great growth", i.e. top wines in an area.

Green: A negative description of a wine made with unripe grapes and/or stalks.

Grosses Gewächs: A German top quality label of a dry wine from a top estate.

Halbtrocken: medium-dry wine in German

Hangover: dehydration and poisoning from over consumption of alcohol resulting in a headache, sensitive stomach (possible vomiting) and lethargy. Shouldn't have had that one for the road, should you?

Herbaceous: the aroma of green leaves, shrubs or herbs, which adds a layer of complexity to the wine.

IBU: International Bittering Units. A scale (roughly equivalent to the European Bitterness Units (EBU)) which represents the bitterness of hops in beer (it's rather complication but you get the gist).

Ice Wine: wine made from frozen grapes. Ice-wine in Canada and Eiswein in Germany.

IGT: Indicazione Geografica Tipica: the lowest ranking of the 3 Italian wine categories (DOC and DOCG being superior).

Intensity: Refers to both the aroma and the taste. Intensity is a desirable characteristic in both.

International Variety: a grape variety which is grown in nearly every major wine region, e.g. Chardonnay, Cabernet Sauvignon, Merlot.

Jammy: when the smell of the wine exceeds ripe fruit and smells of well cooked fruit, it is described as jammy.

Late Harvest Wine: Wine made from grapes which have been left on the vine later than usual. Often a sign that the wine is sweet.

Long: Length or persistence in the mouth after swallowing or spitting. A desirable characteristic.

Mouthfeel: the textural feel of wine in the mouth, covering body, smoothness, acidity, minerality, alcohol, etc.

Nose: The smell of the wine.

Oak: a watertight wood used in cooperage, which imparts complementary flavours in the wine, e.g. vanilla, toast. Oak barrels are expensive to save money, some wineries use oak chips and oak extract. American Oak is cheaper than French Oak and tends to be used for ageing Cabernet Sauvignon, Merlot and Zinfandel. French Oak is preferred for Pinot Noir and Chardonnay.

Off: If the wine has a fault or is not showing it true characteristics, you say that it's off.

Overripe: Picking the grapes late when you want a dry wine is not good. It leads to excessive jammy fruit and a lack of acidity, which means the wine will be unbalanced. Usually found in hot climates.

Oxidised: If a wine has been exposed to the air too much then the oxygen in the air will alter the smell and taste, e.g. if you try to keep that last glass of wine in the bottle and don't use a stopper, gas or other preservation method.

Peppery: Often a characteristic of red wine, particularly Syrah/Shiraz.

Pétillant: French term for a slightly sparkling wine.

Primary Aromas: each grape variety has its own individual smell. This is the primary aroma.

Quaffing Wine: a simple everyday wine that slips down a treat.

Reserva: Spanish ageing designation for both red (aged for 3 years following harvest including at least 12 months in oak) and white (minimum of 18 months ageing, at least 6 of which in oak) wines.

Reserve/Riserva/Reserva

Terms indicating the wine is a higher quality than the basic (perhaps longer ageing, higher alcohol levels).

Rich: Full-bodied, fruity, intense, flavoursome wines.

Rosado/Rosato: A rosé wine in Spanish and Italian.

Rosso/Rouge: Red wine in Italian and French.

Round: Describes a desirable characteristic of a wine that is well-balanced, with no overpowering tannins or acidity, with a good mouthfeel.

Sec/Secco/Seco: Dry in French, Italian, Spanish and Portuguese. NB Sec in a Champagne is medium-dry; look for Brut or Extra Brut for dry and very dry.

Secondary aromas: aromas in wine which come from the wine making process as opposed to primary aromas (from the grape) and tertiary aromas (ageing process).

Semisecco/Semi-Seco: medium dry in Italian and Spanish.

Soft: A soft wine is smooth, fruity, low in acidity and no harsh tannins.

Sommelier: often found in restaurants, the sommelier will know the wine list and menu inside out and back to front so will be able to match your food with a drink.

Spicy: Some grapes, e.g. Syrah/Shiraz, Malbec, taste spicier than others. The term spice can cover pepper, cinnamon, and other well-known spices. Ageing in wood can also add this characteristic.

Spumante: Sparkling wine in Italian.

Super Tuscans: Tuscan wines with table wine designation because they didn't follow the DOC regulations but which were of premium quality and very expensive (often using grapes varieties from Bordeaux)

Tannic: the mouth-puckering part of wine (like drinking stewed tea) which comes from the grape skins, pips and stems. Together with acidity, it's the skeleton of a good red wine. Tannins soften with age.

Tart: A negative description for a wine which is acidic, sharp and unripe.

Terroir: The way the wine expresses the grape variety, geology, geography, climate, etc.

Tertiary Aromas: smells that develop from the ageing process as opposed to primary aromas coming from the grape and secondary aromas coming from the wine making process.

Thin: A negative description for a wine lacking in body or watery or flavourless

Tinto: Spanish and Portuguese term for red wine.

Trocken: dry in German.

Typicity: How the wine expresses the grape variety and terroir.

Unctuous: describes a smooth, rich, intense, complex wine.

Varietal: wine made from a single grape variety as opposed to a blend.

Vegetal: A subtle smell of green matter is desirable and adds complexity. If it is dominant, then it is not a pleasant characteristic.

Vintage the year in which the grapes were picked regardless that the finished product might not be ready for release for several years

Wine: The alcoholic drink made from fermenting, primarily, grape juice.

Yield: the measure of grapes or wine produced per plant, or per area of vineyard

With Thanks ......

A book doesn't just appear by itself. Without the support and encouragement of friends and family, I wouldn't have managed. So hats off and three cheers to:

Georgie Griffin, Tim Griffin, Sheila Atton, Phil Atton, Mike Tuffin & Matthew Ainge.

The terrific Taste Team: Sean Poole, Maria Giancone , Nick Ryan, Arti Reci, Penny Sullivan, Francis Giordanella

Everyone at the UK Sommelier Association, and especially Federica Zanghirella

Lindsay at Wineware, Daryl at drinksave,

The Georgian Connection: John Wurdeman of Pheasant's Tears, Katrina Smith of Arblaster & Clarke, and the Cha Cha Chums.

Theresa Harrow and everyone at Honest Grapes, Vince 'The Saint' Ferguson

Most importantly of all, I would like to thank Howard Wright for his advice, skills, knowledge, expertise and for being a jolly good guy.

INDEX